Past Poets
– Future Voices

2010 Poetry Competition for 11-18 year-olds

The South & The East

Edited by Mark Richardson

First published in Great Britain in 2010 by

 Young**Writers**

Remus House
Coltsfoot Drive
Peterborough
PE2 9JX
Telephone: 01733 890066
Website: www.youngwriters.co.uk

Foreword

Young Writers was established in order to promote creativity and a love of reading and writing in children and young adults. We believe that by offering them a chance to see their own work in print, their confidence will grow and they will be encouraged to become the poets of tomorrow.

Our latest competition 'Past Poets - Future Voices' was specifically designed as a showcase for secondary school pupils, giving them a platform with which to express their ideas, aspirations and passions. In order to expand their skills, entrants were encouraged to use different forms, styles and techniques.

Selecting the poems for publication was a difficult yet rewarding task and we are proud to present the resulting anthology. We hope you agree that this collection is an excellent insight into the voices of the future.

Contents

Wood Green School, Witney

The Poems

Sailing
**('So we beat on boats against the current, born back ceaselessly into the past'
F Scott Fitzgerald, The Great Gatsby)**

So an ancient promise persuades you over the threshold
for the first time since then, and the gables pronounce little more
than a welcome for the lack of visitors. It is half past noon,
yet it seems twelve hours have sailed by, and the house now echoes
with the sound of sleep. You climb the stairs, and float towards
the bed you knew for so long - words that lay adrift on the air
seep into your mind. You dig your body into the mattress,
press your lips against the pillow. It is an old archaeology now,
not earthy fresh, or bursting with the tang of sea spray
as it once did - it doesn't even feel alive anymore. An afterword
of rain clings to the window. It would have been your rain,
made especially for the both of you, were it not for time's
intervention.
Outside, a wave breaks a rock with its tears. As yards grow into
years, you close your eyes and the bed becomes a boat,
cherished, forgotten, sailing into the dream of a dawn.

Gah-Kai Leung (17)

Rain Poem

Rain is the weather that makes me curious,
What if it doesn't come from clouds?
'Yes it does, yes it does,' say the scientists,
But what if they're wrong?
I love the start of rainy weather,
Icy drops on your hands, just letting you know there will be a
downpour,
Then the joy starts,
The growing noise of water splashes hitting windows and
pavements,
The calm feeling of cold running across your skin,
The wonder of puddle reflections,
And the magical glitter sprays as cars fly through them,
I spread out my arms and face the sky,
So this is what freedom feels like.

Megan Bailes (13)

1

Burn With Me

Burn with me
The matches would chant
Being stupid
And having fun
Is what they do all day
Being set alight
Might be a fright
But to them
That's what life's all about.

Burn with me
The matches would chant
Every day
They would say
Burn with me and
Forever have fun.

Burn with me
The matches would chant
Look at the colours
Blazing red and orange
Sometimes yellow and blue
But the best thing they can do
Is chant
Burn with me
Burn with me
For evermore.

Chelsea Snowling (12)
Attleborough High School, Attleborough

Mind

In it, there is mind,
Mind's deepest fears forges anger,
Mind's deepest love forms joy,
Together they form spirit
Spirit is us.

William Ord (11)
Attleborough High School, Attleborough

2

In The Forest

As I enter the forest
I can see
Only five feet
In front of me
You would not notice
It was night,
Because the moon
Is so bright.
Nothing in the forest
Has changed,
Except the colours
Have been exchanged.
Squirrels dance a jig
Somewhere on a high twig,
The owl silhouetted
Against the moon,
Loops the loops
As it swoops.
It watches me creep home.

Sophie Kirkman (11)
Attleborough High School, Attleborough

My Simile Poem
(Inspired by 'The Writer of this Poem' by Roger McGough)

The writer of this poem is
As chatty as a parrot
As sneaky as a fox
As annoying as an elephant
As cuddly as a gorilla
As mean as a lion
As cold as a polar bear
As sweet as a kitty
As cute as a dog.

Gabriella Jade Shepherd (11)
Attleborough High School, Attleborough

3

Old Man To His Wife

I am not yet so old.
That I cannot remember,
Before the years weathered us.

I still see roses in your cheeks,
And the laughter in your eyes.
Your soft, small hand in mine,

The memory of the sun,
Burns me like your kiss,
Our hot skin close in summers gone.

The same moon shines on us,
Our faces may have changed,
But I love your every line.

Beautiful always, though we are old,
Your hair now silver, your heart pure gold.

Catherine Mitchell (17)
Attleborough High School, Attleborough

Smells

Smells of spring
Flowerbuds popping out
Leaves starting to open

Smells of summer
Hay almost ready
Corn being cut

Smells of autumn
Misty mornings
Musty leaves

Smells of winter
Ice and cold
Mulled wine and mince pie
And Christmas coming.

Georgie Harris
Attleborough High School, Attleborough

4

I Like The Noise Of . . .

I like the noise of music,
Beat and tune.
The rhythm and tone.

I like the noise of raindrops
Falling on my head.
The coldness and wetness.

I like the noise of fast cars
Roaring past
The squeaky squeak
The wheels make.

I like the noise of footballs being kicked
And the referee's whistle.

But I don't like the noise of my auntie's voice
Calling me to get out of the car.

Chelsea Bolton (12)
Attleborough High School, Attleborough

When I Finally Can

If left to describe you was me
I would not compare you to flowers
Nor to sky so blue or clouds of white
My love for you is more than this
But I know I mean nothing to you
Winds can howl and rain can pour
Sun may shine and breeze may cool
But you are more than the great outside
You are something that fills me with joy
Others cannot fill my heart like this
But until I die my love won't wander
I have hope you will love me one day
But it is said I should not show love for another man
But the day will come when I finally can.

Laurence Grunbaum (17)
Attleborough High School, Attleborough

5

The Jealousy Within

I envy the lotus in which you grace,
The way in which you stare,
The expressions upon your face,
Your cheek, your lips, your hair.

The sun glistens on your soft skin,
Why does this love compare to a battlefield?
Love like this should be a sin,
So protect me with thy shield.

The tension between us can be cut by a knife,
These temptations are tearing me apart,
Why live a life of such pain and strife,
Damn me and my wretched heart.

So to you, my Heaven and Earth,
Leave me be, and let thy rebirth.

Benjamin Marum (17)
Attleborough High School, Attleborough

I Love Thee

I see thee in a beautiful sunset
Hair glistening in thee sun
You are like a white dove,
You make me glide through air.

I will make thee mine
You are my rose
You are my life
My heart is yours forever.

Beauty, extravagance, love
You have it all
You are like playing with thee fire
Through thick and thin,

We shall always have one another
There is no other.

Jamie Garwood (18)
Attleborough High School, Attleborough

6

A Mother's Love

Shall I tell thee how I love thee so . . .
Since the seed of life was first sown
And seasons three they did pass.
I cradled thee to my breast tight,
Warmth in my heart thee did ignite.
A delicate, precious sign of hope,
As a snowdrop peeping through the winter snow.
Thee is like a precious gem, ruby, emerald, sapphire.
And like thee have a gem forever in a ring,
I shall have thee forever in my heart.
Thee smile. Thee laugh. Thee beauty.
And as thee will grow, I promise to protect thee.
Come rain, come snow come storm, come sun.
Thee will always be the most important one.

Amy Stanton (18)
Attleborough High School, Attleborough

Tears Of A Rose

It hath been three years since you left my side
Yet the pain is still there, a knife between my ribs
How I love to be held in your arms again
Lose myself in your smile
Every day I shed a tear that I still live
And you, my love were taken away
Every night I pray that I sleep evermore
And I can hold your soft palm again
Like a black rose, I wilt, without you there to love
With every petal that falls, my heart breaks
If there is no one left to catch me when I fall
What reason have I for trying?
Dear father, why was it you that they chose?
Leaving me here, forced to be alone.

Chloe Payne (17)
Attleborough High School, Attleborough

7

My Simile Poem
(Inspired by 'The Writer of this Poem' by Roger McGough)

The writer of this poem is
As fast as an F1 car
As tall as a tree
As crispy as a chip

As clever as a fox
As angry as a lion
As wobbly as jelly
As energetic as electricity

As hot as the sun
As sticky as glue
As solid as metal
As clean as a diamond.

Piers Stephens (12)
Attleborough High School, Attleborough

On A Shelly Beach

Seashell
Whistling in the wind
Floating in the water
You always sing
Lonely, sweet and shy
All on your own
Someone will find you
And love you in their home
Carry on singing in their home
Now you are a part of a family
Don't brag, just sing
Your favourite song,
Ding, ding, ding.

Ellie Drake (12)
Attleborough High School, Attleborough

8

The Staring Sun

It shines in the opening of the school gates,
Birds are singing high in the trees
Hedgehogs are curled up in the sparkling sun,
I sit on the grass praising the sun,
Watching it twinkle with sparkly sparks,
A star appears above me,
Daylight has gone,
Darkness has come,
Thousands of stars have turned up all sparkly above me,
I watch till dawn when the stars have gone,
Dust has come and I have to go,
This is why I left this poem for you.

Alice Ablewhite (11)
Attleborough High School, Attleborough

My Shell Poem

I have this shell
It sparkles when I look at it
It's beautiful in every way
It has loads of beautiful and detailed patterns
They are all different shapes
Some are heart-shaped
And some look like a shark's teeth
And it has a spiral topping
It makes a whooshing sound when you put it to your ear
I love my shell, it's wonderful.

Jordan Duffin
Attleborough High School, Attleborough

Key

The key was made near the sea,
The key-maker gave it to me,
He gave it to me near a quay,
But where is the key meant to be?

The key keeps shining gold,
And it always feels cold,
The key has some holes,
And it wants to score some goals.

William Rutland (11)
Attleborough High School, Attleborough

My Scissors Poem!

Scissors, scissors snip my paper,
Cut me off I'll see you later.
Cut me once, cut me twice,
I'll be snipped and would have been sliced.

Oh scissors, scissors trim me up,
Before I overlap and get creased up.
Shame on you scissors, your blade is so sharp,
You leave me in pain as much as a shark!

Jack Watling
Attleborough High School, Attleborough

I Have A Dolphin In Me

I have a dolphin in me
It swims and dives
It twists and flips
It plays and tricks
It leaps and jumps
It dances and wiggles
It giggles with glee
I have a dolphin in me.

Lauren Swann (11)
Attleborough High School, Attleborough

Pot Design Poem

Rain falls and crumbles
On the corrugated iron roof
Like rice grains
From the field's yield
Crumble and tumble
On the tarpaulin
In the harvesting season.

Megan Lotarius
Attleborough High School, Attleborough

I Remember

I remember when it was soggy and I was alone and scared,
A figure coming through the fog, I see my dad
I feel warm even though it's cold outside.
I remember his big thick arms,
I remember his smile.
I can remember he was such a hard worker.
I remember his warm feeling inside and all around.

Jordan Sims
Attleborough High School, Attleborough

The Funny Hamster Verb Poem

I have a hamster in me
It sleeps and plays
It scoffs and runs
It jumps and rolls
It snuggles and squeaks
It climbs and dances
People think it's funny.

Siriwan Morfoot (12)
Attleborough High School, Attleborough

11

My Simile Poem

As crispy as a chip
As wiggly as a jelly
As hot as the sun
As cheerful as a clown
As choppy as your mum
As chatty as a cockatoo
As fishy as a cat.

George Reynolds (12)
Attleborough High School, Attleborough

My Simile Poem

The writer of this poem is
As tall as a bear
As sad as a donkey
As energetic as a biker
As happy as my family.

Troy Cromack (11)
Attleborough High School, Attleborough

Fraya Flower!

O flower tub, o flower tub,
O please hold my loose tooth.
If the tooth fairy comes and gives me a flower,
I will definitely give it to you!

Holly James (11)
Attleborough High School, Attleborough

Teenagers

Ready, set, go.

We are runners,
We are on a race,

The route *we* run for us runners is
An easy one.

It laps the old mountains and ducks graffiti dreams of the sky.
It balances on a tight rope,

Some of us fall . . .
Into a pool of maroon,
But some of us go on, heat tearing us from the inside.

The route jumps through the playground of slides,
Swings and climbing frames;
Some will fall, some will land but all will be scraped.

It wades through the rivers of chemicals
Some will be engulfed and lose their way
Choking, spluttering and coughing.

But the route has already gone.

The route tumbles through fog and smoke,
Offered sanity by clown's yellow smiles
Some will be tricked by the clown

But some will see through the make-up

But then the fog lifts,
The sun comes out

And *we* runners are the casualties of the circle.

Katherine Heslop (15)
Bishop's Stortford College, Bishop's Stortford

The End Of A Son

The sky pounds at the sun,
A sonic boom of colours.
It seems the star has almost won,
The sky fighting back with nothing but wisdom.

A rainbow of sound,
The wind howls, at the possibility
Of death, destruction of the ground.
But still it fights, eager to survive.

The tides are turning,
The moon writhing in its blanket of light.
Hammers of water bash and churn
The rocks of land once glorious.

But still fights the sky.
Eager to deny the end of days.
The clouds soar to new highs,
As the sun draws ever closer.

The soil begins to part,
Like something biblical.
But a god did not start
This apocalpyse of wrath.

An unforeseen glitch
In the warring skies,
The moon arises like an itch,
Uniting the sky with hope.

The satellite rises with strength,
Only to learn of his failure.
The moon cries with a wrench
Of the broken planet it couldn't protect.

And so it moves on,
To find a new planet, to call its son.

Jack Alden (13)
Blatchington Mill School, Hove

14

Untitled

There's a sleepover in town,
If you listen really carefully you'll hear
I'm not allowed to go
But it sounds like fun
I imagine they're playing games
I wonder what they'll play
Maybe pillow fights
Or dress up
Or pick a game out of a bag
Or a favourite of mine
Truth, dare, double dare, kiss, commando, promise
And maybe end with something random
I don't believe it, my mum's let me go
We're telling stories now,
Horror 'too scary'
Romance 'ahhh'
Or bedtime (snore)
We can watch movies on TV
Oh silly me it's a cinema
We've turned my mate's TV on really loud
We've got popcorn and pillows and sweets
We're watching a film
It's funny and romantic
But really gross as well
Tucked up cosy with my BFFs having cuddles
Mum comes in
'Bed,' she yells
We all reply
'Just because it's a sleepover doesn't mean we're gonna sleep'
Night, night (or not).

Shannon Borrer (12)
Blatchington Mill School, Hove

15

The King Of The Jungle

All was silent in the deep, dark wood,
Nothing stirred, nothing uttered a word.

But somewhere down deep below the ground,
Something made a hissing sound.
Something with claws, something with jaws
Something with big, black, hairy paws.

He lifted his head to the moon and growled,
He spread his paws like a lion, proud
With one sharp bound he leapt on the rock,
The little mouse reeled with shock.

With no warning, a stampede broke out,
All of the animals rushing about.
Quickly, like a gathering storm,
The chase for life began to form.

The birds flew up into the air,
The foxes ran here, there, everywhere!
The fish delved deep to their watery lair,
As the king of the jungle rose up like a bear.

The king's eyes alight with wonder,
Stood still and began to ponder
He crawled back to his underground cave
And thought of the way he should behave.

All was silent in the deep, dark wood,
Nothing stirred, nothing uttered a word.

Ellie Edwards (13)
Blatchington Mill School, Hove

16

A Dancer

A dancer is an inspiration to me,
She shimmers in the deserted studio, she stands out.
She blinds and astonishes everyone by her fluidity and perfected movements,
Her smile is a delight to the world and brightens many people's days.
The girl's lips are like a ruby-red rosebud and have a glossy scarlet tint,
Her twinkling eyes are a luscious green.
Her eyelashes are like a thick bold canopy draping over her satin eyelids.

The soothing piece of music drifts through her head, relaxes and comforts her.
This elegant dancer is astonishing, beautiful and she radiates perfection.
The bun in her hair shows her sweet touch with a plaited French braid.
Baby pink ribbons in her golden, silky locks brighten her face,
And add to her innocence.
Her figure reflects on her stamina and strength.
It is slim and lean, a refined muscle machine.

The music slowly fades . . . and the spotlights dim in the evening fiery sky night.
Her pirouette travels down to the smooth surfaced floor and she gradually ends her performance serenely.

Emma Walker (13)
Blatchington Mill School, Hove

17

Snow

The air was frosty, with a sharp winter breeze,
The lake in the darkness had started to freeze,
The ice crept across like clouds in a storm,
And on the trees, delicate icicles formed.

The white clouds gathered in the brisk, cold air,
Children looked to the skies, still nothing was there.
Frost seeped across the ground like a snake in the grass,
Ice clung to the dewdrops, the cold spreading fast.

The changes were subtle, yet still they were there;
The trees were shivering, their branches were bare.
As the world grew silent, and all were asleep,
The flakes began to fall, thick, fast and deep.

The world was transformed to a shining white hue,
Sparkling and shimmering; yet still the snowflakes flew.
A sugar dusting turned to a thick, soft coat;
Snow swirled across the night, the world was smote.

They opened their eyes, their minds were aglow,
They stared out the window at the wonders below.
It came to their lips, the simple cry of, '*Snow!*'

Iona Rose (13)
Blatchington Mill School, Hove

Snow Poem

Snow fell like icing sugar being sprinkled out of the sky,
Cheers of happiness filled the air as snow sprinkled out of the sky.
Hats and gloves came out as snow sprinkled out of the sky
Snow fell like tears running down a cheek,
Oh, how we wish it would snow for a week.
Higher and higher and higher it rose,
Oh, how we love it when it snows!

Emily Knight (13)
Blatchington Mill School, Hove

18

That Is Them All

Travellers
Of the sky
Leaving again

Criminals
Covering
All of their tracks

The weepers
Not always
Sad, but they cry

The dancers
Moving like
Delicate swans

The stairs - they
Lead to the
Gateways - to light

They are lots
Everything
That is them all.

Rochana Johnson-May (13)
Blatchington Mill School, Hove

19

I'll Take You Through Meadows

I'll take you through meadows
Great Oaks will shadow
The sun from your face
As we start to pace
Along grassy banks
And give great thanks
To the sun for this day
To throw our cares away.
Through fields we'll run
No, I won't poke fun
At the leaves in your hair
As it blows in the air.
I'll take you to a place
Where we can forget time and space.
We'll sit on hay bales,
Race snails,
Tell great tales
And just hope the farmer won't catch us.

Milly Gill (13)
Blatchington Mill School, Hove

Goa Is The Place To Be

Goa is the place to be,
With beaches and fantastic views to see.
Every day is something new,
Adventures glare, including canoe.

Goa is the place to be,
With walk-in markets it's just right for me,
Billboards as high as the sky,
Tourists from all over the world say 'Oh my!'

Nia beach has a crystal-blue sea,
Now I know Goa is for me.

Desiree Colaco (13)
Blatchington Mill School, Hove

Slumming It

Mountains of rubbish,
Bottles, wood, glass,
Paper, metal, rotting food,
A putrid aroma fills the air,
People scavenging through the rubbish,
Their noses covered,
As seagulls and rats do in England,
Just to earn their daily rice.
And survive slum life,
They are considered the lowest of the low,
Looked down on, pitied and despised,
But nothing is waste,
Everything reused,
Recycled,
We think our lives are so much better,
But we with our throw-away culture,
We should learn,
As we are killing our planet.

Elspeth Goacher (13)
Blatchington Mill School, Hove

My Poem!

Out in the park, when it was really dark.
Playing with my friend, round the bend.
From my house, there was a mouse.
I tumbled over, near a Rover.
Still at the park, but not so dark.
My friend Daisy is really lazy.
Also my friend Sam, looks like a man.
We went back to my house,
Then saw the same mouse.
Then came my cat, the mouse hid under the mat.
And fell in a big hat,
We went in my room and watched Brum.

Faith McNab Thompson (12)
Breckland Middle School, Brandon

21

War Is Not A Game

Gagging, sniffling, withering in pain,
I'm trying to escape from this dreadful place.
Never coming back,
It's over.

I can't stagger through this anymore,
The agony,
The torture,
The misery,
Death is coming to me,
To someone.

It's not worth it,
They're dying off one by one,
I think I'm next.

I told you, quick, gas! Gas!
It's coming.
He's drowning, sinking, choking,
In that thick pool of gas.
That man - he's a goner,
The poor beggar,
He's there spluttering in my face.

I'm bemused, what if that was me?
That man,
The snarl of his haggled cough
Vomiting violently the thick gas, blood, froth,
Spitting it out was the last thing he did
Before he was loaded on the pile,
With everyone else.

What if that was me?
My vitality is weak,
As I limp on, shed
The weight of my body,
Feels like ten ton.
My muscles worn away,
But I carry on with
The rest of my stamina.

Our vulnerable bodies shaking exaggeratedly
My veins stick out,
With anger and stress.
I have fought for you, yet I get nothing back?
People died for you and they get nothing back?

You say they get pride dying for your country
That's rubbish.
That man died for his country but believe me
It's not worth it.

But I will tell you one thing:
All is unfair in love and war.

Jade Nadine Whybrow (12)
Breckland Middle School, Brandon

What Am I?

I've been here for a far-reaching time
I am above a cold river
Water flowing under
People walking and running over
I hear talking and footsteps
What am I?
I am usually made of wood, brick and metal
So what am I?
Oh and did I mention cars, bikes, buses
And lorries drive over.
I see ducks, boats and an elegant swan.
I am above a river long
For a time
Water flowing under
And people running across footsteps.

I am a bridge.

Dion Griffiths (12)
Breckland Middle School, Brandon

No Place For Children

Staggering through sludge, coughing up blood,
Pain is unbearable we tried to escape death.
Shells and flares stalk as we bolt hastily to safety -
The fear of death provides energy.
Holes in our boots, marching slowly every step brings pain,
We stepped into hell; the souls of the dead still haunt us,
Every cut, scratch and injury can be felt excruciatingly,
But that will soon be over, we leave it all behind.

'Get down! Masks on!'
Struggling to get on our masks
One of our men - too slow,
I think to put him out of his misery,
Cries, 'Gas mask!'
We hesitate,
I turn, can't bear the sight,
A sea of green, shrouds my eyes,
His face imprinted in my mind, I turn to walk,
But he leeches on to my foot,
I pull away but it doesn't help -
I stand helplessly.

What would you do if a dying friend
Begged for survival which could not be given
Would you sit and watch as he died?
Or would you give your life to save his?

Would you follow the trail of dead?
And throw him on?
To be displeased by the blood and mucus that pours out his lungs?

You would not sit pleasantly in your house knowing
What these soldiers
Sacrificed for our country?
To give you freedom and pleasures of your simple life?
Let me tell you!
The war is no playground -
Certainly no place for children!

Oliver Attfield (13)
Breckland Middle School, Brandon

The War Of Thriller!

Sick with chest complaints
Skimming and scanning our way to safety
Surrounded with thick green gas of no mercy
Our time is nearly over
'Gas! Gas!' I yelled, one man was too slow for his mask
Assist him lads to put his mask on
No, too late the chap has breathed in the thick green gas.
The man is dying - going to the world of no return,
I can see him choke, cough, sneeze in pain, he can't breathe
I watch him die in my arms
Spitting out blood with lungs full of gas
They're aiming, they're shooting, they're blowing away our land,
And taking away our lives.

This is my mystery of the thriller
It might get worse, I don't know, but I care for our lives
I wish they would stop and think how painful this is
Why do we have to be foes? This is not right
The horrific mud slicing away our feet
Our boots have shredded to hundreds of pieces as if rats were in
Our boots
The mud is covered in blood that you can't see a thing
I hope that this is a nightmare
I wake myself up; I'm still in the war
I feel the tears rolling down my cheek,
I wish a heavy wind could blow away my fears and the gas,
The rain for a shower, or even the sun to dry away the mud
I know all this will one day come to an end
The only way to stay alive is to be still because the bullets are just
Shooting everywhere
So this is my question for you
'Would you like to die for your country? Would you?'
Dulce ET Decorum Est?

Malcolm Wandera (13)
Breckland Middle School, Brandon

25

World War I

We feel laid up, exhausted, can't stand straight, each step forces us
To choke.

We're trying to get back through slimy soggy mud, marching
All the way, getting to safety.

We are so tried and weak we walk like
Drunken men and we keep tripping over and
Losing our boots, the bombs exploding
And gunshots shooting; the gas-shells dropping behind us.

'Quick boys, gas masks on boys.'

We are still struggling to get our masks
On but one of the members is struggling
To get it on, coughing and crying
Slower and slower he is getting.

We can't see through the green smelly smoke
Getting our masks on and where are you boys?
But finally we get our masks on.

The soldier is dying from the green gas all in
His lungs, he is coughing and trying to outrun
The gas.

I'm so sad that we had to
Stick him on the wagon and watch
Him die, still breathing green gas in for about
Four seconds, he is dead, so we walk, so sad we could cry.

When he's already dead, green gas is still coming
Out of his mouth and nose, his hand still in mine.

If you were in this situation what would you do?

Jordan Dicks (12)
Breckland Middle School, Brandon

The Monster

Lurking in the big dark caves,
Do you know what the monster craves?
Maybe children, maybe dogs,
Maybe antelopes, maybe frogs.

He has big yellow eyes,
And thick hairy thighs,
Great big claws,
On the end of his paws.

He sleeps during the day,
His snores are heard from miles away,
They shake the ground,
While he sleeps asound.

He wakes up at night,
To give all a fright,
The monster from the cave,
Gets ready to misbehave.

He chases the pet cats,
And wees on doormats
He turns the bins upside down,
Scattering rubbish throughout the town.

Just before sunrise,
He hides from waking eyes,
Back to his bed,
To rest his mischievous head.

Jack Field (12)
Breckland Middle School, Brandon

The Seasons

Spring is the first season of the year,
Easter time is nearly here.
Sometimes in May it's Mother's Day,
The cold from winter shouldn't stay,
Jingle jangle of the wind chime,
Spring feels like a happy time.

Summertime is really fun,
Playing outside in the sun.
It's a great time for a barbecue,
Family visits to the zoo.
We get six whole weeks off of school,
That's why summer is really cool.

Autumn is when the leaves go brown,
They're really crunchy on the ground,
Lots of rain decides to come,
Staying indoors isn't much fun,
No more playing at the park,
Autumn's evenings get too dark.

Winter brings lots of snow
Frozen ponds are where you shouldn't go,
Christmas time is nearly here,
After that it's the new year,
People build snowmen that are silly,
Wintertime is really chilly.

Jordan Mann (11)
Breckland Middle School, Brandon

I Like School, Do You?

I like school do you?
I like getting up in the morning, apart from Mondays.
I have Weetabix for my breakfast
And a pea of toothpaste for my teeth
I put on my jumper, trousers and shoes
Then on with my coat and out the door.

It takes 15 minutes to get to school
And 15 minutes to get home
That's 30 minutes wasted in Mum's car where
I could be doing my late homework.

I have loads of friends at school, and they all make me laugh
The bell goes at 8.55 and off to the first lesson I go
I like my French, or should I say Francais?
I like my French teacher, he wears a tie
I like PE, running and jumping, but I'm no good
At basketball, and always get hit by the ball.
Off to maths and English, whoopee!
I'm not good at spelling, but I like adding and take away
But not dividing by 8!

After lunch I have more lessons, then the bell goes
At half past 3, it's the end of the day
I go home in the car, homework then watch TV
Dinner, and later to bed.
Goodnight until the next school day.

Courtney Reeve (13)
Breckland Middle School, Brandon

The Girl Inside

A big house stands alone at the end of our road
Is there any life inside? It seems so still and cold.
From year to year a ghostly face appears,
Her eyes are dark and filled with tears.

Does anyone notice her or is it just me?
Do you believe or is my mind playing tricks on me?
Have you seen the face with the dark eyes filled with tears?
How long has she been there, has it been years?

Children in the street playing games without a care,
Bike bells ring, cars beep, clapping games that make them sing,
Giggles and laughter fill the air, apart from the girl who's not
out there.
Does she wish that for just one day that she could be joining in?

I wish she could come out and play but will she just fade away?
Is she scared of what we will say? I don't even know her name.
Is she longing for a friend, bringing her sadness to an end?

The door slowly opens with a creak, the girl inside looks out for
a peep
She steps outside, slow at first, as if weighted down
Her feet move faster, she starts to run, I can't believe that she
has come.
The force is pulling us together,
We met in the middle now we're friends forever.

Gemma Racine 12)
Breckland Middle School, Brandon

Snow

I am on the floor all wet and cold.
I see paws of animals pushing in my delicate skin.
I hear trees whistling in the wind.
I know my life is going to end.
I feel happy watching children playing.
   I'm snow.

 Shannon Turner (11)
Breckland Middle School, Brandon

30

Poem

Out in the park
Very cold and dark.
About to go on the slide,
To ride the experience of a fantasy glide.
While I was sliding I felt the breeze,
I nearly fell off and started to freeze.
My hands felt like icicles,
It started to snow,
My cheeks were all rosy,
With a red healthy glow!
My friends and I kept on playing for a good half an hour,
To be honest I couldn't wait to get home for a shower!
We ran home fast,
But stopped at the road,
Remembering to use the green cross code.
I got home safely,
And managed to get warm.
It had almost stopped snowing,
But we were in for a storm.
Then heavens opened and the rain came down,
But I was so snug in my dressing gown.
I wasn't that tired and was full of beans
But it was time for bed, so I said goodnight and sweet dreams.

Elise Underwood (11)
Breckland Middle School, Brandon

N . . . N . . . N . . . Nervous!

I'm in a gun
I've been in here for 30 minutes
I see my other brothers lining up behind me
People screaming and explosions
I know I bring death
I feel nervous

I'm a bullet . . . !

Bobby Smith (11)
Breckland Middle School, Brandon

31

Is There A Place?

Is there a place,
All love, no disgrace,
Where nobody lies,
And you never die?
Is it too much to ask,
Or is it a task,
To laugh every day
Brush the blues away,
To banish all poverty,
No more controversy,
To accept one another,
Like sister; like brother?
How good that would be,
For you and for me,
For illness to cease,
To live life in peace?
Will that place be found,
Is that where we're bound?
Or must we keep praying,
To find what I'm saying?
And hope that we find,
True peace of mind?

Molly Prentice (12)
Breckland Middle School, Brandon

My Poem!

I am on someone's feet,
I have been worn for two hours now,
I see lots of gum on the floor,
I hear people talking to other people,
I know that the women's feet smell,
I feel worn,
Can you guess what I am?

I am a pair of shoes.

Chloë Rebecca Parrott (12)
Breckland Middle School, Brandon

32

We Are The People

We are all ordinary, close to the same
But different people that play a different game

We are all almighty,
Powerful and strong
We need to learn some things
That is thought not to be wrong

We should see with our heart
Not with our eyes
We should all forgive and tell no lies

We have different religions
No matter what they are
Respect yourself and whoever we shall pass

Black or white, rich or poor
We are going to stand strong for evermore.

Our future is coming without its clock
It's coming so fast that our time is to be forgot

Do you want that?

I wrote this poem so that you should know
That our future is strong wherever we go.

Alicia Alander (12)
Breckland Middle School, Brandon

Who Am I?

I am in a dark gloomy room,
I have been in this room for two days now,
I saw some people looking at a box with pictures and sounds,
I heard screams and guns,
I know that I was terrified,
I feel like I want to move out already,

I am the chair in the corner.

Ellie Woods (11)
Breckland Middle School, Brandon

33

The Bedroom Monster

It . . .
Waits in small dark corners
It hides under my bed
It lurks inside my cupboard
It's not just in my head.

It . . .
Waits until the light goes out
And Mum goes down the stairs
I know it's out to get me
Giving me nightmares.

So . . .
I check in all the corners
I look under my bed
I tightly shut my cupboard
And put a pillow on my head.

But . . .
I know it's in dark corners
Or underneath my bed
Or lurking in my cupboard
Or maybe . . . in my head.

Joseph Smith (13)
Breckland Middle School, Brandon

The Truth Of You

No one knew,
The truth of you,
All this time,
You've been a lie,
Thinking you're great,
But you've been the bait,
Of the media devils,
Hiding from the cameras,
Running from the flashes,
The true you shows in those,
Who fell for your story,
Of all this fame and glory,
You need to be true,
You need to forget,
Everything that isn't you,
You think
That I don't know,
I'm trying to tell you,
You're not the desperate type,
You're failing to be true,
That's the truth of you.

Leah Sanders (12)
Breckland Middle School, Brandon

35

My BMX Dream

Hoffman, subroza, kink
Which bike today?
What to learn?
What to learn?

Hit the half pipe -
One eighty disaster!
Over the spine -
Whip it in the air!

Pedal! Pedal!
Air out the six foot -
Over the railings -
Adrenaline hitting!

Time for the box -
Tail whip -
Quarterpipe, tuck no hander -
And I'm there!

Oliver Scott (11)
Breckland Middle School, Brandon

Beyond The Horizon

As we sail this breathing sloop, I ponder about what's yonder.
Our captain gives a command however I do not see his rough sea-
beaten face, I see;
Dragons the size of mountains with blood-red eyes that pierce
The soul within.
I also see the biggest rum trader cruising the tides.
Its purpose is to be plundered and that's what we will do.
I find a map, sailing the winds, reaching out and grab it it, it reads . . .
The treasure of Blackbeard!
Returning to reality I am looking out on the rolling waves.
There is a curious flapping noise, looking down at my hands
I see the brown parchment of which could only be one thing . . .
A treasure map.

Mark James (11)
Breckland Middle School, Brandon

36

The Bright Night

The sky is as peaceful as a still swimming pool,
Clouds as fluffy as a sheep
And the odd star glowing just enough to be seen . . .
In this bright night.

The birds singing their song
Makes you feel like the day has gone,
And the cat unaware that it is outnumbered by mice
Makes you want to say, 'That's not right . . .'
In this bright night.

Yet everything has its own bad sides so . . .

The bright night can give one damn fright with the king star
Chasing every single other star out of your sight
So it can glow in its own little sky alone,
Yet again like I said at the start
Only just enough to be seen . . . in this extra
Bright night.

Lewis Kent (12)
Breckland Middle School, Brandon

Suddenly Dawning

I sit by the water and what do I see,
A kingfisher glimpsing back at me.

I notice next to him, a fallow deer,
Lapping up the water while the coast is clear.

I wish I was over within the trees,
With all that wildlife surrounding me.

Would you want all these sights to be gone?
If we use electricity like complete morons.

All of this is suddenly dawning,
The fearful fact of global warming.

Patrick Ellerby (13)
Breckland Middle School, Brandon

37

Trapped

I am trapped
Nowhere to run
Nowhere to hide

I am trapped
Darkness is all around me
I can't move

I am trapped
Pure nothingness
Like an empty universe

I am trapped
Help me
Help me please

I am trapped
Never to return
I am trapped.

Connor Clemens (11)
Breckland Middle School, Brandon

Animals

I think I'm just an orange orang-utang
Or is that just me?
I like to climb and jump out of trees.

I think I'm a dancing dolphin,
Or am I insane?
I like to swim and play games.

I think I'm a scary scorpion
Or am I mad?
I like to crawl and I'm red.

No, I think I'm a cat.

Lauren Rose (12)
Breckland Middle School, Brandon

The Eventful Night

It is a creepy night,
Prepare to have a fright,
Whatever you do,
Whatever you say,
It is a creepy night!

It is a wonderful night,
Prepare for a magical delight,
Whatever you do,
Whatever you say,
It is a wonderful night!

It is a party night,
Prepare for the disco light,
Whatever you do,
Whatever you say,
It is a party night!

It's now the end of the night,
And in the fading moonlight,
Whatever you do,
Whatever you say,
I can't wait for tomorrow night!

Dannii Elliott (12)
Breckland Middle School, Brandon

Snow

I'm on the floor; all wet and cold.
I saw soles of shoes flattening my delicate skin.
I heard children playing.
I know my life has to end.
I feel happy watching children play.
I am . . .
          Snow.

Alex Dickinson (11)
Breckland Middle School, Brandon

39

This Is War

The time has come,
To fight as one,
Against the evil,
For the safety of our people,
This is war.

We will fight to the death,
Even our last breath,
For a new world,
Where in our hearts this legend will be held,
This is war.

A new world we live in,
Where there's not a sin,
The war is finished,
Evil demolished,
We have won.

Louise Prince (12)
Breckland Middle School, Brandon

The Present

I'm in a pinky bedroom belonging to a girl
I have been here overnight
All I can see is a girl with presents
I am a big present
I'm a computer.

I'm very, very happy
The girl is very happy
And so are her parents as well
I'm a computer.

But when they have gone
I feel sad
No one to talk to
No one to see
I'm just a computer.

Chanel Milne (13)
Breckland Middle School, Brandon

40

The Black Wolf

A wisp of wind,
A howl in the night,
A black wolf is singing in the moonlight,
A trudge on the soft wet floor,
A black paw on my bare shoulder,
A wisp of wind
And a howl in the night,
As the black night draws ever near,
Daylight slowly disappears.

Sasha Good
Breckland Middle School, Brandon

Untitled

People walk all over me
But I get to see
The beach sometimes
It comes up to my surface
But it doesn't
Last long so I sigh.

Jasmine Farman (11)
Breckland Middle School, Brandon

Barney

I am hanging, waiting at the stables,
I have worked here many years.
Many tall trees cross my path,
I can hear birds chirping in the trees
I know who's coming to see me next
The happiness inside me is wonderful

I am the only saddle on Barney's back.

Chelsea Irvine (11)
Breckland Middle School, Brandon

41

A Courageous Surrender

Isolation on a journey.

Vacant seat beside me, forever poignant
This emptiness gives leave to contemplation:
First love is a beautiful cliché;
Naivety, a sweet misunderstanding.

Engulfed by faraway memories
I feel like a moon entwined
In a celestial dance without any planet.

Yet I'm orbiting regardless, in pointless circles.

My hollow soul begs for the coup de grace,
Yet it's picked apart and I'm left scrambling for sense.

Glimpses of balmy summer nights
Embracing that nascent world together
Delicate pink cheeks flamed with colour,
Succumbing to your fatal kiss.

Journey ends,
Nostalgic memories
Fade away . . .
Gradually.

So reality can begin.

Love is transient and fleeting.
A courageous surrender.

Kate Atherton (16)
Brockenhurst College, Brockenhurst

War

Deep through hallowed halls,
Marched soldiers heedless to broken calls.

Pain, misery, fear and strife,
Punctuated by each glass knife.

With every passing night,
Mind-sick men scurry further from the light.

Their minds into darkness sink;
Masked by scars and skin blotched like ink.

Until insanity is no longer a release;
Just torture that never does cease.

With happy sigh and light heart
They are summoned for the headsman's art.

Sam Fay-Hunt (17)
Cherwell College, Oxford

43

Blood Lust

I dream, I desire to fight
Because I detest enslavement.
So let me hunt, and let me ruin this world.
I am ready for the kill.

Invincible soldiers cry
When death stares them in the eye;
And the dead soldier every time
Falls to the ground as if they were a puppet thrown by a bored child.

More anxious eyes stare at dead trees
And stretched earth
Carnage clings like a disease onto every
Instinct to kill and destroy in a human.

Soldiers; doggedly determined killers
Stalk the cracked skin of earth,
Under a raw orange sky.
They have no time to see
Little stars drifting -
Drifting into a sky clotted with blood soaked clouds

The freckled rain,
Speckles on burning bodies
Ready for the kill,
And identity is forever lost in the savagery of battle.

A supernatural electricity pierces the atmosphere
As guns let rip their thirsty bullets.
The terror I see outside, barely mirrors
The sickening emotions I feel.

Give me your mercy! The earth screams,
But the steady hum of peace is
Just a distant dream. Yes a shadow of reality.
What can stop scorched, angry mankind?

Hurt.
Hurt, under the mango sun
Animal instinct sears through her blood,
Chokes her veins

44

I dream I desire to fight
Because I detest enslavement.
So let me hunt, and let me ruin this world.
I am ready for the kill.

Taormina Locke (15)
Cherwell College, Oxford

Today Is Another Day . . .

I sit by my mum's window,
On the old oak chest,
I peer behind the guarding curtains,
Shielding me from the outside world.

I see the polluting traffic,
The last of the red squirrels,
People enveloped in technology,
This is the changing world.

People walk down the street,
They never say hello,
They'll just carry on,
As if you were never there.

I hear a crying child,
It comes from across the road,
She holds out a hungry hand,
And fixes her gaze on me.

I turn on the news,
Another coffin draped in a flag,
Another bereaved family,
Another war.

The world is changing around us,
In front of our selfish eyes,
Everyone is watching,
But no one steps up to help.

Today really is another day.

Jana Giles (12)
City of Norwich School, Norwich

45

The Beasts

The attack was led,
By old Charles Selby,
Who killed us soldiers.

Then we died, as men,
Floating to the happy clouds,
Snubbed out too early.

And as it ended,
As we flew, the world ended,
As it died, we watched.

Then the end began,
The end of everything,
Everything we knew.

But always coming,
Emerging from the cinders,
Always here are them.

The beasts three, watching,
Events unfold above, as
Everything begins.

The beasts three, always,
A slow, everlasting death,
For all above them.

The first: Medusa,
The twice-born Gorgon sister,
Slain by Perseus.

The second: the Sphinx,
The dead, sandy monument,
Now, alive again.

The third: a Centaur,
The genius of the three,
And leading the end.

Edward Milne-Brown (11)
City of Norwich School, Norwich

46

The Elements

Fire,
The infernal rage
Swarming across the land,
Chasing away all traces of cold and darkness
And never forgiving those who mock him,
For he has no sense of humour.

Wind,
The joker of the skies
Pushing others to do as he wants,
Though they may not want to
And summoning great, vicious storms
Purely for his own enjoyment

Water,
The quiet, calm creature
Always thinking about something
That has never been thought of
And always finding an answer
To even the most complicated query or riddle

Nature,
The immortal entity
Always learning and maturing
Trying to escape
And as immortal
As the trees that represent her

Lightning
The most powerful of the elements
Unable to control himself
He causes grief
Without wishing to
And instantly feeling remorse
Because of what he cannot help.

William Boyer (13)
City of Norwich School, Norwich

47

The Shark

The shark is very, very wise,
He's quick, he's fast,
He has three tries.
He's very rude,
When he needs food.
He finds a fish,
A perfect dish.
He bites the fish's bony back,
And now the fish cannot attack.
The fish has been crunched like bark,
All because of a fateful shark.
Then there's a splash at the surface,
And the shark wishes he was a walrus.
Suddenly a metal knife,
Quickly whisks away his life.
He is now fresh dead meat,
Waiting for people to dig in and eat.

Jack Rushworth (11)
City of Norwich School, Norwich

A Witch's Spell Poem!

Hear me out, listen to me, and I will give you what you need.
1, 2, 3, in the sea all the dreams, believe in me.
No more worries, open yourself and come on out.
Silver and gold, glittery things with the sun or the sea.
All the seasons of the year, come on my lovely dear.
All my thoughts, and all my dreams,
You are the one which I need.
Unicorn horns and rainbow bows, a sparkle, night comes to life.
All the whispers and all the lies,
Come on and let me fly.

Katie Birch (15)
City of Norwich School, Norwich

48

Stories

Piled up high,
solid blocks of colour,
with writhing caterpillars
dancing as words of ancient times.
Evidence of existence.

They are fed
on everchanging emotions.
happiness, laughter, joy.
On curiosity, anxiety, tears, heavy breathing
capturing, engulfing senses.

Processing minds,
they know all your secrets.
They understand and appreciate you,
but only if you appreciate them.

Mahalia Curtis-Lundberg (11)
City of Norwich School, Norwich

The Shining Final Charge

Leading them to battle, to certain death,
Impaction, fear, will it be their last breath?
Go now, before it's too late, ride for glory
Hold your breath now for the end might be gory
The horses are ready, begin the great charge
Be strong, be brave, be fast, you must be hard
Rule Britannia destroy the foe, kill all
If we meet our match let's hope we don't fall
God's on our side, let us charge, let us ride
Attack now! We might win, ride side by side
Damnation, shots rip through the great sky
Everything comes to this, the end is nigh.

As a hundred bodies did hit the floor
And the great Light Brigade was no more.

Jacob Selby (12)
City of Norwich School, Norwich

49

Love

If my love was a food
It would be chocolate cake

If my love was a drink
It would be Coca-Cola

If my love was a flower
It would be a bluebell wood

If my love was an animal
It would be a pig

If my love was a holiday
It would be the farm

If my love was a film
It would be 'The Simpsons'

If my love was a colour
It would be a rainbow-red.

Ben Cussons (15)
Downs Park School, Brighton

Love

If my love was a food
It would be cheesecake
If my love was a drink
It would be a glass of wine
If my love was a flower
It would be a rose
If my love a song
It would be a love song
If my love a pet
It would be a puppy
If my love a new car
It would be a limo
If my love was a colour
It would be a pink.

Chloe Stenning (15)
Downs Park School, Brighton

50

Love

If my love was a food
It would be gateaux

If my love was a drink
It would be a wine

If my love was a flower
It would be a red rose

If my love was a song
It would be a love, love, love

If my love was an animal
It would be a dog

If my love was a holiday
It would be Derby

If my love was a shoe
It would be Nike trainer.

Kieran Clark (14)
Downs Park School, Brighton

Valentine

V is for violets that I would pick for you
A is for apples that are red like your heart
L is for love on this one special day
E is for excellent which is what you are
N is for nature as beautiful as you
T is for together which we will always be
I is for impossible things that you make possible
N is for never-ending love
E is for every moment we spend together.

Jordan Anderson (15)
Downs Park School, Brighton

51

The Food I Love

When I touch you, I feel your smooth softness
Your soft and creamy taste that melts my heart.
You give a squeak as I dig into you
Your little fat ball of creamy rich taste
Your luscious brown darkness makes my eyes pop
My heart beats faster every time we meet
I love the deliciousness you give out
You're a little cloud bursting with flavour
The little lump of dark creamy softness
Your combination with the red strawberries
Makes my heart beat faster till it explodes
Your cocoa sensation hits me hard
You melt, your cocoa glow becomes lighter
You are the one I cannot live without.

You are chocolate ice cream.

Chloe Kirby (12)
Elm Tree Middle School, Lowestoft

To My Mash Potato

You are a squishy hand
Full of life.
Its best friend is succulent fresh gravy
The oozy sound of the masher working.
Like squelchy snow just waiting to be stood on.
The whiff of it just makes you itch your mouth.
Fragile lips far too precious to scold.
Creamy, buttery, they can't resist it.
Waiting underground, thinking you're the one.
Your thickness and creaminess amazes me
And you need such tender loving care.
Your spotty roundness encourages me
To eat you every minute of the day
I can't help myself, it always calls me
I have a confession that I can't see.

Mae-Ling Yeung (12)
Elm Tree Middle School, Lowestoft

Just For You

You bubble and screech inside my microwave.
You shout my name across the kitchen table.
When I see you my belly rumbles.
You lie in wait upon my plate so wide.
You wait on my bowl for me to eat you.
Your hot delicious taste makes my mouth water.
You tempt me with your lovely chicken flavour.
You swim around my bowl like long thin worms.
How come when I stare at you I get tempted.
You make my heart skip a beat, oh I love you.
When I see you I cannot resist you.
If I could I would have you all the time.
You are a pleasure and a sight of delight.
You travel down my throat, you taste so yummy.

Rhiannon Mortimer (12)
Elm Tree Middle School, Lowestoft

Bubbly

Your bubbly body is possible
Your clear clothes cling to your clear body
You live in a giant igloo for life.
Your many hearts gleaming as they ascend.
I have friends who are thirsty and boiling.
You make people giddy and fun.
You're like ice melting as I carry you.
We are friends for eternity now.
You can be lifeless and lively at once.
You zing down my throat like a waterfall.
You're like a cheetah prowling me for life.
You have a voice but decide not to talk.
You're still but you can be energetic.
But you are all of those marvellous things.

Adam White (11)
Elm Tree Middle School, Lowestoft

53

Dream Come True

You are a river of juice in my mouth and I love
Your green skin that sparkles in the sun
You are silky and smooth
Every time I bite you, I hear a lovely crunch
You smell fresh like you have just been picked and I love
Your taste that makes my heart stop beating
You are my one and only
I hear your lime-green heart beat, every time I come near
You are so delicious, I can't stop eating you
You are one of the most important things in my life
You are like Heaven but better
You make me speechless every time I see you
I never want anyone to take you away
You are my dream come true.

Lauren Palmer (11)
Elm Tree Middle School, Lowestoft

Beauty

I love your shiny, heart-shaped, freckly face.
You lay in your bed until you get picked.
Your voice is sweeter than a sugar cube.
Your bumpy texture makes me go crazy.
You are a river of warmth and I love.
Your ruby-red cheeks which are radiant.
You are always sweet and never sour.
You smell like a scorching hot summer's day.
Your best friends are cream and melted chocolate.
Your little green hat fits you perfectly.
You're a rose-red, memory foam mattress.
Hopefully you will never rot away.
I'm never too busy to spend time with you.
You're a definition of beautiful.

Rebecca Prior (11)
Elm Tree Middle School, Lowestoft

54

To My Pizza

The glorious scent crawling up my nose
The stuffed cheese inside the tender crust
It is the bubbling cheese I chose
It is the food I just must eat, I must!
The velvety pizza is all to me
It has the best three layers in the world
In a treasure chest and I have the key
The shape of a circle and it's been curled
It calls out to me and I get drawn in
It is the mood you want in a nice meal
It is repellent to the glistening bin
If I got offered it, it's a deal
As enjoyable as a theme park ride
I love it more when large and also wide.

Jordan Boyd (11)
Elm Tree Middle School, Lowestoft

My Dearly Beloved

Attracting me from the couch you begin.
The excitement of seeing a leopard,
'Cause you're the rainbow covered with colour.
Your topping is sunlight from summer so,
You are incompatible to winter.
You are the autumn leaves floating downwards.
Your sparkling snowfall, white and superb makes,
Me jump up and say, 'Please give me some now.'
Your lovely blend is the best ever treat.
I discover people licking their lips.
You're a volcano, spilling everywhere.
You smoothly slip down the back of my throat.
After I hear the slurp of spaghetti.

Amy Webb (11)
Elm Tree Middle School, Lowestoft

Countdown

Dots were running, screaming, laughing.
Blobs were trembling, crying, hugging.
Specks of black were on scooters, skateboards.
Figures laughing, for no reason.
Blobs huddled round dots - they know what must come.
In the hour they had left,
They were to spend it with each other.

Tears were running, not many left.
'It'll be alrights,' were passing around quickly.
Young ones, having fun, they have no worries.
Teachers among them, have nothing hard to do.
Presents scattered everywhere, in our classroom.
Big or small, they all meant the same
We were standing, exchanging mobile numbers.
At the same time, conversations with teachers were occurring,
That weren't to happen again.
In the half hour we had left,
We were to spend it with each other.

Nobody smiling, nobody laughing, everyone suffering.

I took my mate's photos, on my camera.
I ran for the tissues - I couldn't hold them back.
I stumbled into my best friend's arms, sobbing, trembling.
I could not bear what I had to do next.
The boys doing fist-punches, nothing more.
Us girls hugging, not wanting to let go.
'I'll miss you, keep in touch, good luck and goodbye'
These are the words that were ringing in my ears.
My friends and I, walking to the door slowly,
Maybe for the last time ever.

In the minutes I had left,
I was to spend them with my soulmates.

My heart was breaking as I had to say goodbye.
My mates are comforting me,
With faces I might never see again.
I felt sorry for myself -
None of my real friends were coming with me,
To the school that awaited me.

56

Final goodbyes said, walked to my school gate
For the last time ever,
And the pain in my heart grew bigger.
Was I ever to see the people again?
Or this building?

Who knows.

Saskia Tyler (12)
Farnborough Hill School, Farnborough

Me!

Mix in the crying so it turns into
Laughter, a nice weekend with
Grandma, I'm being looking after.

We are in the car first day
Of school, the head is whisking
All the new children into the hall.

Suddenly four brothers are stirred
Into my life, Dad gets married,
He has a new wife.

I start swimming competitively, four
Times a week, add in some
Tiredness, I barely get any sleep.

Leave the pan to cool, use the
Wooden spoon and mix it in fast,
Now I'm in Year 6, the time has passed.

Sprinkle in some summer holiday,
Suddenly I fall ill with
Arthritis, but that's just the way.

Pour four jugs of new uniform, make
New friends, then a pinch of
Happiness, the world is coming to
A mend.

Isabella Wynn (12)
Farnborough Hill School, Farnborough

57

Spring

The snow has melted
The winter chill has gone
With patience for the spring
The sun has finally shone

Springtime has now come
Life's new beginning
The sun breaking through
And the birds singing

With longer days ahead
And not so dark at night
Happiness fills the air
Bringing such delight

Springtime has now come
Life's new beginning
The sun breaking through
And the birds singing

Fresh flowers growing
Blossom making you sneeze
All the fruits ripening
Hanging in the trees

Springtime has now come
Life's new beginning
The sun breaking through
And the birds singing

The lambs in the meadow
Playing in the sun
The chirping of the birds
Announcing spring's begun

Springtime has now come
Life's new beginning
The sun breaking through
And the birds singing.

Saskia Vince (12)
Farnborough Hill School, Farnborough

58

The Dragon Who Ate Our School

The dragon came down,
With all its might
And gave everyone,
A humongous fright.

For starters,
It chomped all the cables,
Next came,
All of our tables.

The giant dragon,
Chomped up our school.
Then washed it down,
With our swimming pool.

Great dragon,
Great dragon,
Great dragon you are,
I share with you
My one and only,
Favourite chocolate bar.

Dragon dragon,
We love you here,
But now you have
To disappear.

Our giant hero
Must depart,
So we're all
Torn apart.

Great dragon,
Great dragon,
Great dragon you are,
I share with you
My one and only,
Favourite chocolate bar.

Ella Caldeira-Hankey (11)
Farnborough Hill School, Farnborough

59

A Telephone Conversation

Monday morning,
Nice and cold.
That morning I wasn't *too* bold.
My breakfast was a little bitter,
But, I did want to get fitter.

Tuesday morning,
A little better.
Even though it's a little wetter.
Rain clouds all above my head,
Wishing I was still in bed.

Wednesday morning,
Bright and strange.
Today I found I have no change.
But even though the amazing sun is up,
That doesn't stop *me* feeling like a teacup.

Thursday morning,
The sun is high!
But clouds are gathering in the sky.
Looks like another rainy day,
Washing all the hope away.

Friday morning,
Very foggy.
And my homework? Now it's soggy.
Yesterday I had to bake,
That is all that I can take.

Finally, the weekend comes!
Got the dentist to check my gums.
Then on Sunday I have my sport,
It includes a badminton court.

It is hard to have some fun . .
So, when can you come?

Llinca Dragan (11)
Farnborough Hill School, Farnborough

Watching A River Flow Steadily By

The heat is hot, as heat should be,
The river is quiet and still.
Reeds whisper and shiver in the breeze
And otters arrow through water.

A fisherman grunts and stares at me,
His face is like a wrinkled prune.
A heron swoops down to the bank where I'm sat,
His eyes, shiny black buttons,
He stares and stares with empty eyes,
Sorrow clings to him.

The water is cold and murky green,
Peaceful, yet merciless, to the weak,
It flows on forever and ever on end,
Never dying, never ending, never feeling.

It ripples and splashes against the banks,
Dragonfly warriors defending the surface.
The waves shimmer like stars on a deep green sky
Like autumn grass, soaked by rain.

In the river fish are zooming
Through the foggy depths,
As quick as bullets from a gun.
Shells along the bottom on a misty,
Murky floor are rainbows of colour
In the depths, briefly shining clear.

Gliding through the silt comes
An ugly pike . . .
Splash! Zoom! Flicker! Snap!

Gone are the fish for now.
Gone are the fish for now.

Holly Smith (11)
Farnborough Hill School, Farnborough

Poison

Thundering paws echo,
Driven by a racing heart.
Panting breaths,
Matted fur,
A wolf bursts from the trees.

Behind him,
Flowing swiftly,
Silently,
Slaying and scattering animals in its wake,
Comes fear and death and hate.

Its cruel twisted hand smothering birds,
Its cold foggy breath creeping into hollows,
Killing rodents in their sleep.

It moves quickly,
Determined,
Rushing through forest,
Under bushes,
Round mountains,
Over seas,
Surrounding and encircling.

With a whimper the wolf collapses,
Breathing poisonous air.
A last howl and his eyes close,
His muzzle drops forever.
Another victim of global warming.

Its cruel, twisted hand melts ice caps,
Kills animals curled in burrows,
And lures the sea over land,
Inch by inch.

Lucrezia Lawrance (11)
Farnborough Hill School, Farnborough

Still Hoping Silently

When will they come?
I'm feeling so weak
Will they ever come?
My future looks bleak

How will they find me?
I am trapped and alone
Under a pile of rubbish
I want to go home

At times I can hear them
Searching the hill
But they cannot hear me
Screaming, however shrill

I remember a time
Before the earth shook
It was quiet and peaceful
But now I just can't look

Upon the planet we live on
It seems so cruel
That so many have perished
Will I be the next to fall?

I can hear them louder now
They must be getting near
Then above I see a light
I portray no fear

At last they have come
I'm feeling empty
Nothing more to give
Haiti.

Amy Baker (12)
Farnborough Hill School, Farnborough

A Mouse's Point Of View

Humans don't seem to have
Any brains,
They always think it's us
Who chew the gas mains.
And they seem to think that
Green stuff is nice,
But I'm sure it's just
Out there to get us
Mice.
But what I don't quite
Get, is
Why those stinky
Dogs,
Get the luxury of a
Pet.
It's like they were born
Just to be fed
And laze around,
While we have to
Scurry and dig
Underground,
It's just not fair to me,
That we have to live without any knees,
And scurry around on,
Four little feet,
Whilst they get the luxury of TV
See what I don't quite
Understand,
Is why they get to be the
Rulers of the land.

Lucy Shearer (12)
Farnborough Hill School, Farnborough

Duos Est Iam Unus

Open space, no one
Around just me,
No hills, no buildings
That I can see,
Then suddenly amongst
All that bare,
There
Galloped as quick
As a hare,
A herd of magnificent horses without a care.

They galloped hard and fast,
No interest in the world
They passed.
They were chestnut,
Skewbald, bright bay,
Golden chessboard, grey,
For every sound they made
Came an answering neigh.

In all my wildest dreams there could have never been,
Such a beautiful, graceful, moving scene.

But then I saw the black stallion,
He was as black as coal,
Tall as a Spanish galleon.

On his back was a girl, the two in perfect harmony,
He the rhythm, she the answering melody,
The perfect orchestral piece,
Duos Est Iam Unus.

Sophie Voase (12)
Farnborough Hill School, Farnborough

African Acquaintances

As I stepped out of the aeroplane
Onto the African plains
Without getting drenched in rain
But being scorched by the red-hot sun
Which was shining high
In the brilliant sapphire sky

As we travelled on the safari
I came face to face with a rather large elephant
I gave it a sugar lump
And it gave me a head bump

Then I came across a giraffe
It gave me the heads up
Because it stood up so tall
And that was all

Next I met an aardvark
I said, 'You are the first I read of in the dictionary
But I have never seen you in a zoo.'

Then I met a hippopotamus
Down by the stream
Talking to a rhinoceros
About last night's dream

As we travelled back to camp
I came face to face with a rather large lion
I was about to ask it
'Have you been fed?'
But it ate me instead!

Alannah Christianson (12)
Farnborough Hill School, Farnborough

Mystery

Thieving dear lives and causing many heart breaks,
Looking over cherished ones fall,
Watching the figures on the horizon reduce,
One by one by one.

Destroying valued landmarks,
Or even just houses of the unfortunate innocents,
Stealing loved possessions,
Like a raging river among the quiet woodland.

I
Kill
Break
Steal
Leave
Heart break
Fear
Create
Hurt
Create peace
Bring pain
Bring tears
Show love
Bring people together
Create memories
Regret.

I am not just death.

I am war.

Emma McClure (12)
Farnborough Hill School, Farnborough

A Horse And Rider

In the hills,
A long moving figure,
Gliding along the landscape.
It's a warm day.
Birds and bees dancing,
Trees swaying with joy.

A horse and rider
Come into view,
Focused on the green carpet
Ahead of them.
The horse raring to go,
Legs moving like a powered windmill,
The hooves breaking up
The soft blanket.

The reins flapping in the wind,
Rivulets of sweat
Making their way down
Her rosy cheeks.

You can see the concentration
In the horse's face
As they move onwards.
To the big orange ball
They race the wind.

Then like a sad watercolour
They merge into the . . .
Beyond!

Zoë Bennfors (11)
Farnborough Hill School, Farnborough

Animal Cruelty

A is for animal testing, horrible but true
    Think of all the animals dying for you
N is for the nausea I feel
    When I see all those animals start to peel
I is for ivory
    The elephant's tusks his to keep
M is for the monstrous hounds
    When the dreaded trumpet sounds
A is for the awareness for the animals' plight
    Don't shy away keep it in sight
L is for life
    That seals have no more

C is for chickens led to their death
    Waiting to be evilly cooked by the chef
R is for rabbits whether they are having fluids in their eyes
    Or being made into rabbit pies
U is for uncaring
    What hunters are
E is for emergency animals dying
    But some people are really trying
L is for loving, caring and helping
    We can stop those poor animals yelping
T is for the torture those animals go through
    We can help those animals too
Y is for you who can make a difference
    So we can end these animals' sufferance.

Grace Charles (13)
Farnborough Hill School, Farnborough

Shadows

They're dark and cold,
They hide from me
And never look at me.
They lie there so still.

I turn away from them
But when I look again, they've got closer to me,
Why do they have no faces?
Why are they cold and black?

They are like slithering, slimy snakes
Waiting to attack.
I turned away from a shadow one day
And when I looked back, it was gone.

They are everywhere you go
On the floor, on the walls,
Behind you and in front of you
Lurking, watching and waiting.

Beware, I said that day,
Don't stare straight at them
Because if you do,
You may never come back.

So now I must go
Don't look, don't stare,
The only thing to do is
Run!

Isabelle Colley (12)
Farnborough Hill School, Farnborough

Sailing

On a cold, windy, autumn's night,
All together with one small light.
Huddled close on a boat,
Tucked up warm as we set afloat.

Putting on my bright lifejacket,
While eating from a crisp packet.
Hunger leading into starvation,
As we sail through the nation.

On a cold, windy, autumn's night,
All together with one small light.
Huddled close on a boat,
Tucked up warm as we set afloat.

Every hour we hear the sound
Of the foghorn above the ground.
Voyaging through lots of caves,
While sailing along with the waves.

On a cold, windy, autumn's night,
All together with one small light.
Huddled close on a boat,
Tucked up warm as we set afloat.

Messages in bottles we must send,
Communication we need to depend.
That we will see our families,
Once we've finished on the seas.

Jess Kelly (11)
Farnborough Hill School, Farnborough

Rail Road

The shining line cutting through the country;
No longer did dirty steam belch out
Like two-day-old snow; today it is as clean as ice,
Reflecting the now bright sun.

Rickety line cutting through the land;
Steam polluting the never-ending sky
Like ink blotting paper; today no different,
Never-ending trek into the scorching sun.

In the distance the sound of cars.
A bonfire was burning nearby, grey
Cotton wool smoke, rising
Into the newly hot air.

In the distance the sight of parched land.
Burnt out campfires, black
Ash covering the ground, settled
From times ago.

People spilled from the carriages, leaves
Blown in a storm, bumping and falling until
The wind finally calmed and the leaves fell, scattered
In all directions.

Empty carriages, one lone soul
Drifting into the back and beyond,
One star twinkling in the darkness,
Until extinguished, never to be seen again.

Josie Buckingham (13)
Farnborough Hill School, Farnborough

Black And White
(A blind old woman speaking through her eyes)

Cherry blossoms grow pink as cheeks,
The ray of sun shines through the azure sky.
The magical glow of boutiques,
The laughs and cheers of children walking by.
All these things so easy to see,
But black and white is what appears to me.

Sacred mountains stand cold as frost,
The early bird wakes to live the next day.
Bees hum around as if they're lost,
Daffodils spread through fields in disarray.
All these things so easy to see,
But black and white is what appears to me.

Keys playing on the piano,
The soft touch of a feather on my nose.
The scarlet sky in the morning,
The delicate pink petals of a rose.
All these things so easy to see,
But black and white is what appears to me.

Trapped in this cruel world we call life,
The burdens some people bear are painful.
Hurt stabs like the end of a knife,
Is life always like this, sad and awful?
Colour is what everyone sees
But black and white is what appears to me.

Nayan Gurung (13)
Farnborough Hill School, Farnborough

The Boy And The Beast

Scattering paws and stomping feet
A boy and his mouse, running round the street
What a wonderful sight
All the street lamps alight
The candles were glowing
While the cool breeze was blowing
But the dark mist hadn't been seen before

All of a sudden, a scream in the night
As the little white mouse gave the boy a sharp fright
It grew bigger and bolder
And jumped right out his hands
Until the big paws
Of the grey beast did land

Just then the boy's face
Went white as a ghost
Like an old, sunken boat
Just after that, the streetlights went out
And the cool breeze shook
The trees this way and that

Shrieks and moans as the rat attacked more
But the boy was quite still, with his dirty wounds raw
His little heart hammered and he let out a cry
He was waiting for help
Or else he would die.

Ellen Murphy (12)
Farnborough Hill School, Farnborough

Oh Wondrous Ancient Tree

Your oak arms travelling so widespread and free,
Your spindly legs digging deep into dark loneliness,
Your huge knobbly body holds everything steady,
Your knowledgeable head disappears into the frozen clouds
Oh wondrous, ancient tree, so old and watchful.

Lydia Steven (11)
Farnborough Hill School, Farnborough

74

The Midnight Swan

And through the darkness I dipped my feet in velvet ink,
Feeling the warm, soft breeze stroking my face.
The substantial moon reflecting in the vast pool,
Making a long silvery streak separate the water.
My foot swayed side to side,
Creating purple blue ripples,
Shimmering and melting into the night air.

Something soft and pure
Drifted into my gaze.
There floating on the surface,
Was Sofia my swan,
Elegantly tossing her long neck,
Showing off her ghostly white wings.

An armful of white blossoms,
Lightly rested beneath her breast;
She flapped her wings excitedly
Feathers darted everywhere,
Joining the floating blossom.

She sung farewell,
Gliding off into the darkness,
Until the moon and I lost sight of her
And I knew deep down this was the last goodbye . . .

Katherine Gasperi (11)
Farnborough Hill School, Farnborough

Untitled

Standing on the top of an emerald hill,
Breathing in fresh air as butterflies soar.
I see a river flowing fast, filled with diamonds.
I turn and run to help it on its travel north.

In the corner of my hazel eyes I spot
Daisies jiving to the rhythm of the wind,
While heather smells as sweet as buttercups.

When near the water's edge there is a sudden breeze
It feels like water is rubbing against my cheeks,
Through the mirror of beauty, seaweed sways
Pebbles as dark as coal, anchor at harbour.

Golden swastikas sit at the bottom smiling
Letting the water be on its way north.
Snails attached and hanging on for dear life
As the water forces its way through the bends of death.

I can feel the spirit of the water,
Smell the fresh water and see the rainbow trout.
Scales just like a rainbow of jewels fit for the king.
Big blue eyes gaze up at me and away,
While looking down towards the ground of green moss
I notice the daisy is filled with rays of the sun.

Ibby Kingdom Mueller (12)
Farnborough Hill School, Farnborough

Snow Day

I opened my window, all I could see was soft shimmering snow,
I rushed downstairs and got the phone call, school was off!
I burst out with excitement ready for a day, full of fun.
As soon as I got outside the snow came pouring into my wellies,
I felt a burst of excitement at the thought of going sledging,
I walked up the steep but steady hill,
With one fierce push . . .
I was down before you could blink!

Rebecca Niblett (11)
Farnborough Hill School, Farnborough

76

Champion Runner

I sprint past the trees,
Faster than any other animal,
I am a champion runner,
Of the world.

Soon I slow,
I'm losing energy,
My muscles are tiring,
I'm about to break down.

Suddenly I leap,
I'm soaring through the air,
The wind in my face,
The ground down below.

Within moments I land,
On top of my target,
On top of my meal,
My claws sinking in.

I'm so hungry,
I rip him apart.
Although I'm in the middle of nowhere,
I've had another victorious win.

Bethany Voller (11)
Farnborough Hill School, Farnborough

As Sad As A Whale

It was as black as night
And he was as sad as a whale
The snow lay like a white carpet on the ground
The town was as silent as the ocean
With snow falling as soft as feathers
But yet he was as sad as a whale
The town was as white as icing sugar
It was as beautiful as a rose
But yet he still was as sad as a whale.

Polly Spence (12)
Farnborough Hill School, Farnborough

77

That Sweet, Sweet Night . . .

As the cotton clouds daydreamed by,
They disappeared into the never-ending sky.
As the sand under our dry feet whirled past,
The galloping hooves travelled fast.
Whilst the whistling wind bashed the waves,
And the beach ball was saved.

The galloping hooves scattered sand,
Over the children playing on the land.
One's reflection bounced off the shimmering waves,
Scaring those children who are not so brave!
Like a lion, the wave came rushing upon the shore,
A rapid swish and a frightening *roar!*

Then all went silent, I looked around
Nothing to hear, nothing to be found.

A giant silhouette dived out of the sea,
It gradually came closer, closer to me.
It floated under the sea like a predator searching for food.
I started running backwards and then fell to the ground.
I found myself upside down.

It was all a dream that sweet, sweet night
It certainly gave me a fright!

Anais Dibben (12)
Farnborough Hill School, Farnborough

Loves And Hates

My favourite animal is a monkey
Because they're really fun and funky
Spiders are a creature I hate
Always hanging on my garden gate
I always enjoy watching TV
While I sit and eat my tea
I think 'The Simpsons' is the best
It's much funnier than the rest
My other favourite is Harry Hill
I laugh so much it makes me ill
Shooting is a hobby of mine
Although I prefer it when the weather is fine
I really hate Brussels sprouts
But I love going fishing for trouts
In summer I like playing cricket
I enjoy bowling at the wicket
I hate tidying my room
Just the thought fills me with gloom
I love to eat sweets and cake
Especially the ones that I make
Can't think of much else to say
That's enough for today.

Beth Cowan (11)
Farnborough Hill School, Farnborough

What Does Snow Mean?

What does snow mean to you?

White icing sugar dusted over the trees.
Cold stuff covered up to your knees.
Sledging, playing, snowballs too.
All of these are so fun to do.
This is what it means to you.

What does snow mean to me?
Shovelling the whole street for 50p!
Watching as the white icing sugar fills up,
The whole street.
As it glistens, as it sparkles,
It still weighs heavier than ten tonnes of charcoal!

What does snow also mean to me?
Watching the birds go hungry in the tree,
After all how do birds find worms,
When they squirm, in the snow?
But worst of all parents home! Uh oh!

After all that,
Here's a little fact,
I don't mind snow as long as it knows when to go!

Laura Phillips (11)
Farnborough Hill School, Farnborough

80

Dreams

I close my eyes,
Wrap myself in the crisp clean sheets,
I close my eyes,
And slowly wander to another land,
I close my eyes,
And slowly wander to my own little land,
I close my eyes,
And I am in a place where,
The wind is blowing but I'm not cold,
The sun is shining but I'm not hot,
It will snow when I want,
Like a snow machine on demand,
But it will stop in an instant.

This is my land,
No one can touch it,
No one can judge it,
No one can feel it,
I feel the thrill of things happening around me the way I want it.

This . . .
. . . is my Dream Land.

Caitlin Jearey (13)
Farnborough Hill School, Farnborough

The Tiger, The Sea

In the distance, on the edge of the shore are
The impatient waves.
Oh so fierce and strong, storming closer and closer
Like an angry head teacher on the prowl
For that disobedient boy.

I loiter here with my sisters, water crawling down my cheek,
Rain hurling down from the heavens
Every drop like a bullet against my face.

Emeralds and diamonds cascade off the sea,
Showering the sands with razor sharp shimmering jewels
Creeping closer and closer like a tiger stalking his prey.

I yearn for home now; the tempestuous carnivore
Is advancing up the beach at a tremendous speed
Like a racing car nearing the finish line.

My feet are rooted to the spot like potatoes in a vegetable patch,
And I feel the waves swarming round my bare feet
Like flies attracted to sweet sticky honey.
I am stuck like glue.
No way of escape.

Eleanor Selby (11)
Farnborough Hill School, Farnborough

My Hero

My hero is special to me
My hero is kind.
In my heart there she'll be
Yes in my heart there you'll find
My hero and me.

She is always there to look after me
When I am all alone
And yes she'll be
Looking after me till I am fully grown.
My hero and me.

Now I'd better tell you
Who my hero is
Well my hero is my . . .
You'll have to wait and see.

Well I guess I have to tell you
If you really must know
My hero is my . . . *sister*
And I love her more than snow!

Isabella Esposito (12)
Farnborough Hill School, Farnborough

83

Spooky

Branches knocking windows
I turn around
There's nothing there.

Shadows lurking
Floorboards creaking
With my every step

Faint noises
Cobwebs hanging
I'm all alone

Blankets of dust
a shiver down my spine
It's a nightmare

Spiders everywhere
I shout for help
There is no reply

Thoughts flash through my head
I'm terrified
I'm trapped *forever!*

Hannah Sutherland (12)
Farnborough Hill School, Farnborough

School

Here I go, up the hill,
To the big, dark scary school,
I know no one,
I have no friends,
I am alone.

I sit in the classroom,
Waiting, waiting
Everyone seems to know someone,
Not me,
I am alone.

Natasha Lee (11)
Farnborough Hill School, Farnborough

 84

Wandering Into The Sea

The sun was glaring at the Earth,
Golden sand shimmering below.
I could hear people happy in their mirth,
While running to and fro.

The blazing hot sand under my feet,
I could stand there forever.
Looking at where the sky and Earth meet,
I love this place more than ever.

I walked towards it and saw how frothy it was,
A soft and foamy feeling.
I realised that the closer I got,
I could feel a cold sensation, a sort of tingling.

I dipped myself in and began to swim,
My body felt numb.
I couldn't feel a single limb,
I couldn't even wiggle my thumb.

I could see something in the sea, what was it?
'Argh!' I screamed . . .

Tanzim Thaphader (11)
Farnborough Hill School, Farnborough

A Snow Poem

Crunch, crunch, crunch
Goes the snow beneath your feet
'Ouch!' you exclaim as the snowballs hit you.
Whoosh! goes the sledge as it slides down the hill.
'Hi!' say your friends as they come to meet you.

Drip, drip, drip
Go the icicles on the roof
Splat! falls the snow from the trees
Crash! go the snowmen falling to the ground
Oh! sigh the children as they see the wonderland melt away.

Hannah Phillips (11)
Farnborough Hill School, Farnborough

85

Water

Sparkling diamonds cascading from the sky,
Tiny droplets of dew.
Water in its different forms.
Smoothly running through.
Stream and river,
Sea and lake,
Babbling brook,
Spitting on your face.

Cool and refreshing,
Pure and clean,
Spray or puddle,
Splash or wave,
Various shades of aqua-marine.

Then angry and vicious,
Huge raindrops start . . .
Rain like bullets hurling from the sky,
The heavens have opened,
And those below will never stay dry!

Lucy Collins (11)
Farnborough Hill School, Farnborough

My Snow Poem

Snow is falling all around
It doesn't even make a sound
It covers every branch and tree
And in your eyes so you can't see.

Children playing here and there,
Snowballs flying everywhere,
People sledging down, down, down,
As they race towards the town.

Crunch goes the snow,
Whoosh goes the wind
'Yay, say,' the children!

Katie Fidgett (12)
Farnborough Hill School, Farnborough

86

The Beauty Of A Cat

No human could understand,
The greatness of a cat,
Their graceful walk,
Or their eating habits.

They prance around their territory,
Acting like they're the boss,
Ready to pounce on any intruder,
Not letting anybody get into their garden.

Then they come inside,
Moan at you a couple of times,
You give them their dinner,
And they sniff it then just walk away.

Off they go to their favourite place,
Jumping up the stairs and racing down the corridor,
They jump up onto your bed,
And stretch as far as their paws can reach,
Curl up into a ball and fall fast asleep.

Laura Smolinski (11)
Farnborough Hill School, Farnborough

The Colours Of The Rainbow Are The Colours Of The Heart

The colours of the rainbow are the colours of the heart,
Each one is significant and has a special part.
Red with passion.
Yellow with happiness.
Orange with kindness.
Green with envy.
Light blue with sadness.
Dark blue with rage
Purple with pureness.
The colours of the rainbow are the colours of the heart,
Each one is significant and has a special part.

Therese Page-Tickell (13)
Farnborough Hill School, Farnborough

87

The Granny That Never Grew Up

There was once a granny
Her name was Mrs Franny
And she was the granny
That never grew up

When the snow fell
She gave out a yell
Made a snowman
That sneezed
And had knobbly knees

A fort that was disheartened
By wearing a tartan
And she was the granny that never
Grew up

She was very old
With a heart of gold
But she was the granny
That never grew up.

Sophia Page-Tickell (11)
Farnborough Hill School, Farnborough

Spirits

People running . . . running away.

Deafening screaming; the sound
Reaches my ear.

Dying. People lying there just *dead.*
Just dead.

Destruction
Rubble, wood, metal.

Blisters, blood, pain.
Death, destruction
Death, destruction.

Katie Curtis (11)
Farnborough Hill School, Farnborough

88

New School

Well you see I joined a new school,
And it is very, very big.
I have really nice teachers,
Even if some of them wear a wig!

The problem is the homework,
So much every day.
It mounts up extremely quickly
'I hate it,' I say!

The lunch is lovely,
It really fills you up.
You get your lunch and pudding,
But you never get a cup!

You always get the same feeling,
When the end of school bell rings.
You run down to your locker,
To collect all your things!

Hannah Mansell (11)
Farnborough Hill School, Farnborough

Niagara Falls

I'm behind the greatest waterfall in the world,
The Grand Niagara
Its horseshoe shape,
Its strength,
Its power.
It's Mother Nature's daughter,
It will never end,
It will always flow and move
Like a never-ending dance.
It will always tumble
Like a rolling gymnast
It will always show the power of the Earth,
It is nature at its most high.

Heidi Small (12)
Farnborough Hill School, Farnborough

89

Dreaming

When time gets rough and all around,
I want to escape life with a bound,
When my burden is as heavy as lead,
I jump up into my nice warm bed.

I close my eyes and begin to soar,
Through the clouds, I so want more,
I want to stay up here forever,
Go down to earth, stop flying, never.

But then someone comes to call my name,
I come back down - it is a pain,
I once soared high above the earth,
It felt just then like a whole new birth.

When I grow up I may return,
But maybe I need to learn,
Life is not just flying high,
Sometimes you really have to try!

Verity Stuart (12)
Farnborough Hill School, Farnborough

Sweet Shop

One day I was walking back from school,
When something caught my eye,
A sweet shop down the road, how cool!
I gave a hungry sigh.

Maybe I could go and see,
I have some money to spend.
And it won't make me late back home for tea,
Because it's practically round the bend . . .

Wow this sweet shop is really great,
It's got everything you can eat and more,
And the time is only half past eight!
I was meant to be back by four.

Kailey Aliyar (12)
Farnborough Hill School, Farnborough

9o

My Snow Poem

Snowflakes flutter from the sky
Icicles dangle way up high
Children shout with great delight
Playing in the wintry light

Robins search the snow to feed
Squirrels scratch around for seed
Snow keeps on falling down
The trees are no longer brown

Bright pink wellies slide around
Scarves are dropped on the ground
Snowballs fly through the air
Ending up in people's hair

Snowmen appear on the ground
Dogs are running round and round
The air is full of jolly laughter
I wish this could last for ever after.

Rebecca Cramp (12)
Farnborough Hill School, Farnborough

Something's Coming

Turning the pages, scanning down,
Something's coming, something brown,
Those eyes, those eyes so green,
Staring up at you, staring up at you.

Leaning back, to wipe your head,
Sees its chance, and leaps ahead.
Now on your lap, it starts to buzz,
You have no choice, reach out a hand . . .

It's on the pages, settling down,
Something's there, something brown.
Those eyes, those eyes so green,
Are closing, peace at last!

Ellie Travers (12)
Farnborough Hill School, Farnborough

91

Dancing Disaster

They twist, they twirl,
They lift,
They jump,
Like elegant butterflies dancing in the sky!

Suddenly her foot slips,
Sending her sprawling,
Across the hard mahogany floor,
Her partner flying with her.

Slowly pulling herself back up,
She places her two feet firmly on the ground.
She grabs a hand of her partner,
Dragging him to his usual position.

Her feet still sliding,
She anxiously moves,
Towards the centre with her partner
Where they replay their music again!

Jessica Kelly (12)
Farnborough Hill School, Farnborough

Autumn

The leaves fell from the honey-toned trees,
Each one a different shape and colour,
The trees were on fire but now they're going out,
And now they're as bare as ever.

Each leaf is as wrinkled as the shed skin of a snake,
And is always curled up as if it's going to sleep,
Their skin is so crisp and delicate to touch,
It's amazing how they've lived their life, but now it's time to stop.

The trees are cold and lonely but the ground is very crowded,
Even though the leaves are gone there's still plenty of life,
Now it's time for sleepy animals,
To get ready, for a long winter's night.

Jessica Cramp (13)
Farnborough Hill School, Farnborough

Us

His gormless face upon me,
His heartbroken eyes,
His mouth as wide as a great wall,
The future is out of his sight.

He takes a few steps closer,
To see if I'm really there,
His hands go up to his mouth,
All he can do is stare.

I point in the right direction,
I walk with him at my side,
I smile happily at the realisation,
That he's smiling nice and wide.

We get to know each other,
We smile all of the time,
But we always seem to remember,
Our special little rhyme.

Addie MacGregor (13)
Farnborough Hill School, Farnborough

The Sign Of Winter

I wait, and wait, but nothing comes,
I long to see some snow upon the ground,
I do so wish that soon will come a couple of snowflakes.
Yet I wait.

There will be no green grass but a duvet of snow at my feet.
The trees will glisten like stars in the night's sky,
The puddles will be stilled with a layer of slippery ice,
And there will be icicles hanging from the door handle.

Oh look, over there a tiny snowflake,
Bold and clear, it floats down like a leaf.
Soon there are dozens of them, drifting down one by one,
Finally snow has come.

Lauren Whittle (11)
Farnborough Hill School, Farnborough

93

My Poem On A Certain Someone . . . ?

In life you go through difficulties
Easy and hard
And you need to make the right choice
Otherwise life is a windy path

You're sitting at home wondering
How life would be
If you treated people
Respectfully

So now you have learnt your lesson
Treat people with respect
Because the coolness will wear off
Your life will be wrecked

Otherwise this will happen again
And eventually the path will end
Leaving no sign of home . . .
Practically a *dead end* . . .

Liberty Burnett (12)
Farnborough Hill School, Farnborough

All It Took

The beach huts are coming down,
No one going through town.

I wonder why and what,
And is it the girl with a pot?

People fleeing with fear,
I know that it is near.

I look around scared,
I wonder when and where?

I turn away for a look,
And that was all it took!

Emily Ross (12)
Farnborough Hill School, Farnborough

94

The Rushing River

Listen . . .
Hear the careful rush of the crystal-clear river
Slowly . . .
The water flows, gently moving, as the wind quickly blows it along
See . . .
The beautiful birds flutter their wings whilst glaring at the silent rush
Delicately . . .
Fish swim, gliding through the icy depths in search of food
Look closer . . .
You may see the fire-orange fish, the snow-white swans,
Grass-green frogs or the colourful dragonflies circling the lake . . .
Watching over like an angel
Magnificent . . .
Sun smiles and waves hello,
I walk along, I want to join in, dive, the beauty of nature, I swim
Admiring all that was done well.

Christina Maloney (12)
Farnborough Hill School, Farnborough

Flea And The Dog

Around my ear
Across my tail
Under my legs he goes.

Around my neck
Over the other ear
Over my nose he goes.

Tickle my feet
Make me sneeze
Itch, itch, itch.

Pass him onto my human
Itch, itch, itch.
Now it's his turn to see a vet.

Yippee!

Sophie Peterson (11)
Farnborough Hill School, Farnborough

95

The Football Match

Oh yes, today is the day
Where Chelsea and Manchester are going to play.
Everyone is excited, jumping up and down,
Acting as if they have gone to see a clown.

The game has started, the whistle has blown
There is Sir Alex on the edge of his throne.
Chewing his gum and looking rather worried,
Already surprised that he has not scurried.

John Terry has scored his third goal.
Leaving Man U in a deep dark hole.
Frank Lampard now shows off too much,
And ends up having to use a crutch.

The paramedics now come on,
People shouting, 'Carry on!'
It seems as if Rooney's down
Now who will get the golden crown?

Sangeeta Rijal (11)
Farnborough Hill School, Farnborough

Me Poem

My bedroom sits in front of me,
My music playing loudly.
My bedroom door is open wide,
So come on in and look inside.
My teddy bear is watching me,
Someday waiting to be free.
Finally I've got my phone,
It's the coolest thing I've ever known.
My DS lies waiting to be played,
With moving drawings that I've made.
My dog is lying on the floor,
Which made me want to talk some more.
My life is amazing,
Which makes me want to do some lazing.
My family is quite funny,
As the weather is quite sunny.
This is me and my amazing life!

Tara Byrne (11)
Farnborough Hill School, Farnborough

The End Of The Snow - Drip Drop!

Winter came
Cars remained,
Sun disappeared
The snow reappears
Drip drop.

Hats and coats
Made by goats
The snow from clouds
Hits the ground
Drip drop.

School closed
Cars slow,
Snow melts
No time to sledge
Drip drop.

Natasha Redknap (11)
Farnborough Hill School, Farnborough

Me!

Add a bunch of brown hair
And Mum and Dad's support
Don't forget my favourite sport
Add happiness and laughter in the bowl
Let it settle ready to roll
Pour the craziness
Don't forget the messiness
Sprinkle a bag full of smiles
Leave the mixture for a while
Crush blueberries for blue eyes
Make me as set as apple pie
Bake me for 9 months
Wait until cool.
Then I can go to Farnborough Hill
My favourite school.

Georgia Christie (12)
Farnborough Hill School, Farnborough

98

Afghanistan War!

Who are the real heroes?
Nobody knows,
Not football stars,
In their shining cars.
Soldiers saving lives
Feeling so very deprived . . .

Who are the victims?
Nobody knows,
Children disappointed not getting what they wanted.
Those who died of starvation and war,
Beginning to wonder what it was all for . . .

We hope the soldiers' efforts will not be in vain,
From far away we share their pain.
I hope this war will come to an end
So the world can make peace and all be friends.

Lydia Baldwin (11)
Farnborough Hill School, Farnborough

Friends

True friends are few and rare,
Deny that, don't you dare,
In times of need, trouble or pain,
They help you stay perfectly sane.

To have spoken your mind and not been scared,
It's nice to know that someone cared
Memories that you spend with them are happy and good,
They're always there to lighten the mood.

Time passes by ever so fast,
But thoughts and friendships will forever last,
And though our friendships may bend and break,
An apology is all that it takes.

To make things better again.

Malka Reuben (12)
Farnborough Hill School, Farnborough

99

Me And My House . . .

My house is filled with roses
My bedroom's the size of a whale,
My teddy bear sits on my bed,
My books are all over the floor . . .

I love to eat in my room
I hate the smell of paint
I always stroke my cats
I never stroke my snake . . .

The bathroom always smells
The floor is always clean
The rooms are full of cobwebs
The doors are off their hinges . . .

My life will go on
And on and on in misery . . .

Hannah Barnardo (11)
Farnborough Hill School, Farnborough

My Beach

Clear blue skies above my head,
Golden sand beneath my feet . . .

Smell of fresh air and seawater fills my head
Taste of ice cream on my tongue . . .

Sound of the waves,
Crash on the rocks . . .

Children laughing
Joking,
Playing . . .

Bouncy yellow ball in the sky beats down on me,
Keeps me warm . . .

Year after year we come here,
And always marvel at its beauty . . .

Gemma Glasscock (12)
Farnborough Hill School, Farnborough

100

Past Poets, Future Voices

I hope for my future voice to be, not just a mediocre melody,
Which deteriorates from your memory once another song is played,
But to be an operatic solo, that never expires and hits number one in
every chart.

My words are to act like that catchy jingle on the radio that never
exits your mind,
Or that legendary piece of art Beethoven once made.

I long to deliver harangues that inspire, and leave thoughts hanging
over your soul,
Along with those thoughts, a smile, that only came about when you
heard what I had to say.

Like the birds in the sky,
There's always a leader, darting through the ocean above,
Instructing the others, on how to make the beautiful patterns.

As we watch their performance from down below,
We realise that a leader's job is to set an example,
Just as all the past poets set for me.

Tara Acton (15)
Francis Bacon MCC, St Albans

The Homeless Streets

Streets, streets, streets
There is no warmth in the streets
Streets, streets, streets
The cold surrounds the streets
Streets, streets, streets
The people walking in the street
Streets, streets, streets
And the lonely man in the street
Streets, streets, streets
That is me.

Philip Cocker (15)
Fred Nicholson School, Dereham

Life In The Bombing Post

Tick-tock, tick-tock,
Boom, bang, boom.

All is silent except for rats scurrying all over the
Dead bodies.

Bang, bang, bang,
Cough, choke, cough.

Soldiers shouting,
'Gas, gas, gas,'
Struggling to get their masks on.

Puke, puke, puke
Dead, dead, dead.

Frightened because our friends have died

Scream, scream
Crack, crack, crack.

Large footprints glistening in the snow

Tick-tock, tick-tock
Boom, bang, boom.

Leon Scott (15)
Fred Nicholson School, Dereham

I Can't Escape

I can see barbed wire.
I can hear screaming.
I can't see through fog.
Rats run through my legs.
I can't stand the smells.
The blasts are so loud.
The darkness is coming.
Time is running out.

Conner Raven (15)
Fred Nicholson School, Dereham

You Make Me Feel

You make me feel proud
Your eyes are as blue as the ocean,
I try not to be loud
You're much hotter than sun lotion,
You are as beautiful as the moon
I'm so lucky to have you,
I'd like to marry you soon
I love your Kung Fu fighting.

You're so pretty, men are staring
I love your juicy lips,
They must love the clothes you're wearing
They're as lovely as party dips,
Your skin is as smooth as a bed
I love the way you play the guitar,
It's just as nice as your lovely head
You're as fast as my Jaguar.

I love the way you dance
As I grow I feel for you more,
I'm so glad you gave me a chance
I just want to put you in a drawer,
I love your silky hair
My love for you is so true,
You're my little teddy bear
I just want you.

Luke Herrington (13)
Gillotts School, Henley-on-Thames

Love Is No Easy Thing

Love is no easy thing,
The words don't mean anything,
His 'I love you' is meaningless
When you see him loving someone else.

Love is a hurtful thought,
When you realise how much he fought,
To keep it secret, away from you
And now I am here in need of rescue.

Love is a roller coaster,
But sometimes he is such a boaster,
When he finds someone else,
And leaves me to fend for myself.

Love is like a war zone,
Many girls left all alone,
Because of his selfish love,
Instead of white there flows a red dove.

Love is patient so I will wait,
For that one lucky special mate,
To whisk me off my tiny feet,
No random man in the street,
But a handsome prince all for me!

Jasmin Bonello (12)
Gillotts School, Henley-on-Thames

Love Is Beautiful, Love Is Kind

Love is beautiful, love is kind
Love is bountiful, love is blind
What will I say? What will I do?
How do I express my love for you?
Love is here, love is real
How will I say how I really feel?
Love is hard, love is true
Please oh please can I be with you.

Bryony Walker (12)
Gillotts School, Henley-on-Thames

 104

You Killed My Soul

Every touch, every hug, they were all lies.
Bang! Stomp! On top of my heart,
I loved you, and then you take me by surprise,
Please just go, I need a fresh start.
You killed my soul.

What have you done?
Why did you do it? Why?
Please just go, don't you see, you've won!
That's all you've ever done, 'Lie! Lie! Lie!'
You killed my soul.

You were my shining light,
To guide me on the way,
Sometimes I think this gives you delight,
So listen, you hurt me, you poached my heart, you won okay!
You killed my soul.

You were my love, my life, my heart,
But that's gone now, it's gone forever.
Look what you've created! 'A piece of abstract art!'
Whatever, wherever, whoever,
You killed my soul.

Yes you, you killed my soul!

Katie Thomas (13)
Gillotts School, Henley-on-Thames

The Trenches

Gunshots coming from all around me
Lives are thrown away in seconds
Soldiers crying, others dying
All just want to flee
Clouds of blood
Killing, slaughter, murder
Death.

Matthew Breeze (13)
Gillotts School, Henley-on-Thames

105

It Grows Inside Me

Why do you always do this?
You give me a beautiful kiss
Then leave me all alone
My skin as white as bone

Just you don't really care about me
If only you could see
How much I love you
Whatever you think times two.

As it grows inside
I can only hope and try
But soon that day will come
When I will not have won

I do not have long
Until I hear the song
As this cancer grows inside me
And now it's time to leave.

Alyssia Smith (12)
Gillotts School, Henley-on-Thames

106

Perfection

As the clock strikes midnight,
We run through this countryside, out of sight.
Together, hand in hand, we're in love,
Our love is pure, like an angel or white dove.
I lay in your arms, surrounded by this dark abyss called night,
The moon and stars are our only form of light.
We watch the stars, and like diamonds they twinkle, glimmer
and shine,
I tell you, I'm so happy that you're mine.
For without you I would be lost,
My heart would be cold and lonely, covered by frost.
You pull me closer in this intimate embrace,
We sit in silence for a moment, just staring into space.
Some people say that it's just young love, it won't last,
But I know different, because my love for you is strong and vast.
You turn to me, I smile, and you look into my eyes and say,
Your beauty is in a league of its own, your smile lights up this night
And turns it to day.
You brush your hand, ever so softly across my face,
Its warmth penetrates my skin, and so my heart does increase
in pace.
Seconds, minutes, hours pass, I remain in your arms, but I must
go soon,
As the sun is coming up and we bid farewell to the moon.
We stand as day breaks on this summer's day,
We only say goodbye, there's nothing more to say.
You kiss me, with every ounce of passion in your body, we walk away
I change direction,
I turn to watch you until I can see you no more,
This time we spent together has been simply perfection.

Lucy Reid (15)
Great Cornard Upper School, Sudbury

Love, Bites!

As we make love, he holds me close,
I can feel his passion, it's like an overdose.
I look into his eyes; for I see no soul,
As expected, all that one can see is a bottomless pit, a black hole.
I love him with every ounce of my being,
In his presence it feels so freeing.
As if he has no morals and no rules,
He does not dare, nobody he fools.
I know he has a secret, a secret I now know,
And tonight this secret, he will show.
He caresses me,
As we share this ecstasy.
I feel a piercing pain,
One that will lead to my personal gain.
As the blood drains from my face,
My heart stood still so did time and space.
For when I awake again, I will be immortal,
As if I crossed the divide of normality, and our love was the portal.
He has made me strong,
He has given me power, I know together invincible, we belong.
Fore I am a vampire now, at this time and at this hour,
My life's just begun, a new door's opened like a fresh
blossoming flower.

Shanice Brooks (15)
Great Cornard Upper School, Sudbury

 **108**

Howl

I howl to the moon at night,
I climb to the highest of mountains, out of sight.
Pale skin, cats' eyes, the heart of a wolf, I wasn't born this way,
I would rather not have this secret to hide, but this way I have to stay.
My nails as sharp as blades,
When I hunt, I have no reason; my soul turns as black as the ace
of spades.
Take me in your arms and make me real,
I want a real life, normal is what I want to feel.
Turn this she wolf into a girl, a human being,
A human loving, a human knowing, a human seeing.
I move swift and sharp, like a dart,
Every move I make is perfection from the start.
You can hear my howl for miles and miles on end,
And yet I'm still alone, with no one to call my friend.

Gaby Raw (16)
Great Cornard Upper School, Sudbury

109

Street Life

The streets are lethal like a gun owned by a baby,
14-year-olds screaming out, 'Someone please save me,'
You can die from the companion that you're sharing
To the colour of the clothes that you're wearing,
But when youth die it's just put to one side,
Nobody knows about the boy who died
Or how much the parents cried,
It all gets washed up like an angry tide.

Drugs and money are the cause of death,
Young people caught up because they don't know what's best,
They feel unliked like an empty treasure chest
They know what they want but it doesn't come off their chest
So they join a gang, get a knife and put it in a chest,
Once you're caught up you're not getting out,
Like a spider in a spiderweb, you're not getting out
Even if you cry, even if you shout
One you're in there's no getting out.

Matthew Vrioni-White (14)
Hailey Hall School, Hertford

War Poem

Soldiers feel hurt and sick without to sleep,
Soldiers stand in the trenches and see some man dead
In mud and drowning,
Rats eat them at night,
And I can see lice on him and us too,
I can smell dead bodies, gun, gas
We climb over the trenches, run and shot,
Bomb behind us,
Become dying and dead on the ground and blood out,
My eyes going shut and I can see in my eyes
That I see black of in my mind,
We at up of the sky and gone,
War end.

Kathrene Borland (13)
Heathlands School, St Albans

110

War Poem

War in France.
Soldier blood died
Five bombs
Lots soldiers, trenches.

Letter come from family
And friend
Makes me cry, I love
All family and friend.

I want be live not,
Be died.
I love all family and
Friend,
If I be died.

It mean I will fly up,
Can't see any more,
Family and friend,
And I not like see,
Our family and friend,
Cry over me
Died.

Thomas Wooding (13)
Heathlands School, St Albans

Romance

They say that romance is dead.
Well, that's not what I've been led;
After ten years I still get woo'ed.
Put your tongue away, don't be rude!
True gents are worth their pound,
Face it, there are not many around!
My feet are always dry, I get lifted over puddles,
Me and my dream man, everlasting cuddles . . .

Texas Gowman (14)
Heathlands School, St Albans

111

War Poem

Field is brown,
Trees feel drowned
There's nothing beautiful around,
I feel like leaves falling down.

Bullet hit to soldiers,
Rocks are solid,
Soldiers walk to the hill and feel pain,
Many types of blood come out of soldiers
Because of rain.

All soldiers die,
All crosses are tight,
Soldiers are dying,
They are closing their eyes.

War is horrible and a liar,
Soldier look and feel like fire,
Their soul then flies away,
Their whole family feel pain.

Sanna Soomro (12)
Heathlands School, St Albans

Cheating

I am trying to hide my tears,
Giving up, I let the tears break free,
Rolling down my cheeks.
Looking away from him,
Walking away from him,
Acting like nothing has happened.
Footsteps coming closer to me:
'Sorry, I was wrong to do that.'
I want to forgive him but cannot,
Walking away in silence,
The footsteps fading away.

Mia Ward (13)
Heathlands School, St Albans

112

The Welcoming Sun

It was dark,
Rain splattered everywhere,
I stood there alone,
Wearing a long yellow raincoat,
With a hat,
And wellington boots.
I was soaked up to my head.
Rats scuttled everywhere near the pier.
Sea waves were crashing,
Thunder boomed everywhere.
At the crack of dawn,
Everything stopped.
Here it comes,
Sunshine!

Joshua Page (12)
Heathlands School, St Albans

You Are A Star

Shall I compare thee to a sparkling star?
Thou art more noble and pretty:
The sunrise doth light the day and fade the stars.
The clouds blocking your sparkle
The light's on, stars fading
The lightning distracting people from the night star.
Clouds, seasons change
Nature making noises to distract thee.
But thy star's sparkle shall not fade,
Because real stars fade but you are more beautiful,
And the stars will never be more beautiful than you.

Jake Ash (13)
Heathlands School, St Albans

113

A Love Never Broken

A man looks at a woman
A woman looks at a man
A love is created
A journey begins.

A love continues
Until the end of life
Love still lives.

Brandon Scott Gurney (13)
Heathlands School, St Albans

The Shark

The shark silently swimming
Through the azure ocean
Gold sand below

Above sky is grey like the shark
She smells blood
And like a crack of lightning
Opens jaws and snap!

Jacob Hine (12)
Heathlands School, St Albans

Dolphin

Diving and splashing in the sea
In the beautiful oceans all around the world
Near the beaches with palm trees and sunsets

Teenagers playing in the water, splashing all around
Smart, smooth, sleek dolphin, gliding to them
Nice and gentle friends.

Tyler-Ché Thomson (13)
Heathlands School, St Albans

114

The Lion

He stands very quiet like a mouse
In hazel-yellow long grass
Lying like a king.

The sun closes in, heat rises,
He watches the shadow moving
And roars when he finishes the meal.

Xandria Edwards (12)
Heathlands School, St Albans

The Voice Within

I'm scared
It's as if no one cared
I can't speak
My mouth, all it does is leak
Them dirty heartless souls
Have left me with a great big hole
How do I say who did this to me
I'm left standing here on top of a tree
My hair is being blown in my face
I have no hands to help me get out of this place
They took my shoes, they no longer respected
My womanly rights have now been neglected
I have a tree stick for hand
I am no longer in my princess land
My heart it's shattered, all my trust has gone
I was raped for a whole hour long
My body it hurts, I have been abused
They stood there and laughed, why were they amused?
How could they do this to me? I'm such an innocent girl
Whenever I think about it it makes me hurl
I see the birds in the nightly sky
Why am I living my life as a lie?

Yasmin Mulford & Ellie Gladding (15)
Hellesdon High School, Norwich

115

The Lust On Lavinia

A horse ride I was taking
With my love on summer's day
Glistening streams and still skies
Little did I know it would be our last
On our journey we saw deceitful Tamora
With a too-loving moor
He was startled and fled
We joked and toiled of her false love
As we were going on our way
The sons of the whore who came henceforth
She used her silver tongue and told them a lie
Told them murderers were we
Planned on cruelty and vicious torment
Had they not arrived
Saviours are they prove you are my children
My love stricken with blade and fell to the ground
Revenge, hate, confusion and pain
These are all emotions I feel to thee
Took me away, the children of Goths
Beaten and raped they left me
Tongueless and handless
Bleeding in pain, certain death
Marcus had come and found me alive
Who has done this evil this fair day
I spoke but blood for no words could leave me
Nothing but a crow frightener a scarecrow
What will I do, what will I do
There's nothing left
No love, no fear, no hope
Just torment.

Barry Ducker (15)
Hellesdon High School, Norwich

116

Poem

They grabbed me from behind,
I felt so confined,
They threw me to the ground,
And gave me a little pound,
The next thing I knew,
And I didn't believe it was true,
I was raped,
Then taped to a tree in a swamp,
They cut off my hands,
And replaced them with strands,
Then they severed my tongue,
This really stung,
I was hurt and alone,
And I was feeling so prone,
Then my uncle turned up,
And said the word sup,
He then took me down from the log,
And out of the bog.

Luke Dalton (15)
Hellesdon High School, Norwich

Because I Love You . . .

I give you my body, my face, my lips.
I give you my heart, my soul, my spirit.
I give you my passion, my strengths, my weaknesses.
I give you my hope, my dreams, my desires.
I give you my happiness, my fury, my sadness.
I give you my future, my destiny, my fate.
I give you my love.
I give you my everything.
And in return I ask nothing yet everything.
I ask you accept my lips, with tenderness and passion.
I ask you accept my weaknesses, with modesty and acceptance.
I ask you accept my dreams with wonder and enthusiasm.
I ask you accept my sadness, with compassion and care.
I ask you accept my fate, with strength and judgement.
I ask you to give me your love.
I ask you to give me your everything.
Because I love you . . .

Katie Tavender (15)
Hellesdon High School, Norwich

118

Stolen . . .

They killed Bassiarnuss and took his love from me,
I tried to scream for help then I tried to flee,
But they took me to a swamp that was dark and bare,
All I've got now is memories from there,
I was abused,
But they were amused,
They were laughing and joking,
While I was just choking,
I was a toy,
Used for their joy,
They cut off my hands,
And replaced them with strands,
Then they cut off my tongue,
And I wished they were hung,
They were so vain,
They left me crying in pain.

Jack Wright (14)
Hellesdon High School, Norwich

Winter Sonnet

White snow falls over the December town
Robins perch on the holly berry tree
The bare trees covered in a soft snow gown
Children rolling snowballs, laughing with glee
Whilst the fat cat purrs by the open fire
Families sit together, sipping hot drink
Everyone to bed; peacefully retire
Fresh frost over the abandoned ice rink
The harsh cold gust runs down the empty street
The delicate snowflakes float to the ground
What seemed continuous snow, turns to sleet
Happiness of winter has spread around
The soft gentle patter of tiny feet,
Squirrels emerge and spring is here to greet.

Hannah Browes (14)
Hellesdon High School, Norwich

The Trenches

I ran across the field, the wind rushing past my head,
Screams and shouts around me as the first blood was shed,
The Germans stood a while away, guns mounted high,
Shooting at the helpless and watching them die,
They were not real killers, they wouldn't hurt a fly,
But the rule for men over there was simple: either fight or die,
Life seemed so precious yet in a flash it was gone,
The only ones left standing were the bold and the strong,
The weak and the feeble were the first ones to go,
While the others would crawl around keeping their heads low,
So as I ran through that field my life flashing before my eyes,
I was waiting to get hit and find myself gazing at the skies,
Friends were falling around me, lying on the ground,
They deserved a better death than this, being killed without a sound,
I came across a man, blood seeping out of his wound,
I didn't want to admit it but I knew that he was doomed,
I tried to help him but only made it worse,
I know nothing about medicine, I'm not even a nurse,
My legs were aching now but it wasn't going to stop me,
If you're going to succeed in anything to keep trying is the key,
All over I was shaking, absolutely terrified
I knew my family would be proud of my courage even if I died,
I would live in their hearts until their life ended,
Then we would meet in Heaven and our broken relationship
Would be mended,
If I survived this war there would be only one thing that would
Be good,
I had learnt how to treat the world and how we all should,
Suddenly there was an explosion next to me and I thought
My time had come,
I realised that it was a land mine and my whole body went numb,
I could hear sweet music and my vision was a blur,
And that was it, I would die where I were,
But somewhere in the distance I could hear my name being called,
I could hear someone crying too and felt despair as they bawled,
So I opened my eyes and heard four loud gasps,
And the tick-tock of a clock as the seconds passed,
My family were sitting around my hospital bed,

Then my mum said, 'Oh Matthew, we thought you were dead,'
I realised that I had got out alive and then I cried,
Thinking of all the people in this hospital who had sat with their
Loved ones while they died,
Their loss must be so deep,
Sitting next to a dead body and hearing a high-pitched
Continuous beep.

Matthew Seaman (11)
Hobart High School, Loddon

The War

My life had changed
When I heard the news
I had to fight,
To save the Jews.

It all started when
The horror struck
Came flying down,
I was out of luck.

From out of the sky
I could see
There was nothing,
Nothing more for me.

There was a crash,
I saw everything fall
That's when my life collapsed,
And that's not all.

I was trapped,
Pinned to the floor,
Getting dark,
I breathe no more.

Georgia Sargent (11)
Hobart High School, Loddon

The Sorrowful Battle

Mourning and sadness everywhere,
A never-ending stratosphere.
Adrenaline's surging through my veins,
An agonising, pitiless game.
Machinery weighing down in my hands,
Accompanied with an elastic band.
Every time I run away,
I just get flung back for another day,
Of bullets flying past my head
And a painful feeling of definite dread.

It's depressing with all the turmoil around,
And I find it hard to stand my ground.
The screams of dying men ring in my ears,
So I find it really hard to hear.
Destruction is everywhere I look,
Everything I have has been took,
In one fatal, devastating blast,
But I have to carry on as it's the past.
I wish I could escape this place,
Where death and life wear much the same face.

The enemy come back every day,
With a vengeance you can't take away,
They've lost some men but so have we,
They shouldn't be fighting so avidly.
I hope the battle ends quite soon,
I'm filled with guilt but mainly gloom.
The commanding officer doesn't care,
He likes this kind of wild warfare.
I suppose I'll have to stay where I am,
I hope I don't die. *Oh my God,*

Bam!

Ellie Hagan (11)
Hobart High School, Loddon

122

Memories

In my dreams he's all I see,
When the clouds float by,
He watches me,
When the wind whistles through the trees,
I hear his voice,
Calling out,
When the birds sing their cherished songs,
They sing to me,
For him,
How I remember his face,
Full of warmth and happiness,
How I remember his voice,
Echoing in my thoughts,
I remember his glowing blue eyes,
Which moved you like the moon with the tide,
When the doves fly by,
They wink at me,
When flowers start to bloom,
They seem to smile,
When the rain falls,
I wonder if it's his tears,
How I remember his face
Full of warmth and happiness,
How I remember his voice,
Echoing in my thoughts,
I remember his glowing blue eyes,
Which moved you like the moon with the tide,
These are my cherished memories,
A very special gift,
I shall hold them close to my heart,
Always!

Amy Soanes (12)
Hobart High School, Loddon

My True Love

I stood on the path looking at him.
He didn't even cross the road.
My cheeks were red, my eyes were wide,
And he didn't even turn his head.

I was truly invisible to his bright blue eyes.
But he was attractive to mine.
I blush and turn speechless and fall to my feet.
Whenever he comes into sight.

Whenever I sit next to him
Or even on his table.
I dream about our future together,
Having a perfect life.

But I know it's not true
As he never speaks to me
It's all in my head.
We won't be together, forever.

But I might as well give up.
As my one true love
Doesn't even know I'm here.
And he's already broken my heart.

Charlotte Squirrell (12)
Hobart High School, Loddon

War Is So Lonely

Alone, alone, alone
Sitting in a hole
Bangs of fire
Relieve souls to the open
The injured shout
While leaking red water
No place to hide
The screams can always reach you
Even if you're not listening
Waiting for backup
I can see them
Nooooooooo!

Where am I?
What is this place?
Where is everybody?
Where's the light?
Alone, alone, alone.

Charlie Folkard (12)
Hobart High School, Loddon

7.0 On The Richter Scale

This emigration
This seeping of life
Weeps like a wound from a word
Or a knife.

Like the drip of a tap
Or the hourglass sands
Another life lost
As another grain lands.

The fields were farmed fuelling
Life, growth and birth
But there was more to be given
By the life-giving earth.

When the tremors had ended
The dust settled down
Broken buildings and bodies lay in bits
On the ground.

Like the drip of a tap
Or the hourglass sands
Another life lost
As another grain lands.

Holly Hewitt (16)
Holbrook High School, Ipswich

126

Distopia To Utopia

Distopia 2050
In Distopia people live in fear - people start fires, people slash tyres
Noises of screaming, no smiles or beaming
Kept under control, no voting in the polls
There is electric humming and the sound of running
And the distant drumming
Tall sharp spire, gunshots fire, people sigh, people die, people cry
Flaming machines, no one can dream
No careers only fears, slowly tears from our peers
No one sober, over and over - riots every day, not allowed to say
Everything grey apart from fire
One million pounds for a loaf of bread, if you vote for them
you're dead
No imagination in your head, always starving, no one fed,
Down this path you must not tread,
If you do this cut with sabre, blade like razor, years of hard labour
No life to live on thoughts to give, your fate is sealed, at least
it's not real.

Utopia 2110
A wonderful place, with wonderful grace, a lush green land,
Light shines like golden sand, broken by leaves and wonderful trees
Just a glance would suffice for your entire life, chaos runs free
For you and for me
The ruins of Distopia, no more fear, no more guards with their tazers,
Guns and lasers
We made plants grow, we tried so, all the animals are alive
Everything thrives
People now hate electrics, it makes them sick
We overthrew society, we were killed, time to rebuild.

Marcus Breeze (12)
Horringer Court Middle School, Bury St Edmunds

127

The Great War?

The Great War
Some people call it,
But behind the slogans there's something different
All that 'die for your country'
More like die for the Devil
Or
One man -
The important one
Fighting with your friends in the same battalion.

When that pen touches that paper
You sign
Your death warrant
From then you don't have a name
You're a
Uniform
And
A gun
With your friends in the same battalion.

The gas
The horrifying scarring gas
Which bubbles your insides
You're in agony
For weeks
Slowly dying
Never stopping
Pain
You die in vain
With your dead friends from the same battalion.

Thomas Moore (13)
Horringer Court Middle School, Bury St Edmunds

128

The Glamorous Side Of World War I

Seeing your mates
Talking to them
About your family
What you did in the past
Playing cops and robbers
Pretending to shoot each other down
But this is real -
This is war.

Joking about the people
The posh people
In the back line
Saying this food is 'scrumptious'
In their upper class voices
Pretending to be part of the war
But this is real -
This is war.

So when your
Pen touches that piece of paper to sign up
For the war
It feels like you're signing for your family
To save their lives
And your country.
You feel like you're a hero all ready.
You decide - your life.
You're in charge -
What will you do?

Because this is real - this is war.

Matthew Saffery (13)
Horringer Court Middle School, Bury St Edmunds

Faraway Outcast

Cold is the northern wind;
Gusty November dawns;
And chilly December snows.

Heartbreaking, is the cry that echoes,
From far away . . . distant shores.
Alone in this world,
I hear not the ring of sweet words,
Feel not the joy of everlasting friendship,
Nor the warmth of a lover's touch.

Spring is never followed by summer -
Summer never followed by fall.
Winter rules here; forever, eternal.

My nights are dark and dreamless,
Above me the dancing aurora,
Below me; endless ocean waves.

My guide; the evening star;
My light; the eastern sun,
By night; my western moon.
Sunset stain me crimson red;
Sunrise set my skies alight
Let me dream of cloudless, azure skies
And summer roses,
As I sail home
To you.

Heqing Qi (12)
Horringer Court Middle School, Bury St Edmunds

World War I

I remember . . .

The snow falling on the floor
Playing with my friends
Chucking snowballs at them.

I remember . . .

Playing cops and robbers
On the green grass
'Bang, bang you're dead
50 bullets in your head.'

I remember . . .

We signed up for the war
With the same pen
Laughing and playing.

I remember . . .

Jumping in the muddy puddles
In the ditches.
Just like trudging in the trenches.

I remember . . .

Screaming when we were playing
Like a wounded animal
But now it's real.

Sophie Wells (13)
Horringer Court Middle School, Bury St Edmunds

Rain Poem

Rain.
Silent as snow, loud as thunder.
Rain.
Diamonds from the sky, clear as crystal
Smells like a fresh summer garden,
Tastes like a mountain spring.
Like velvet on the skin or knives to the flesh.
Can make you as happy as a cheery robin,
Can make you as glum as a dark storm cloud.
Water from Heaven to wash all away.
Cliffs crumble in its presence,
Mountains tumble in its wake.
Strong as the wind, yet gentle like snow.
Nothing can stand in its way.
Metal cracks.
Rock breaks.
Wood rots.
All are defeated by the water of life.
Rain.

Ashley Ben Wiggins (12)
Horringer Court Middle School, Bury St Edmunds

The War

Crisp dry desert
Being trampled by
The soldiers' heavy boots.
Walking out of base
Into unknown territory.

Sounds of gunshots
And screams of peril.
Fellow soldiers waiting for the war to end.
So they can go home to their families.
Just standing there waiting,
Hoping to survive.

Charlie Clayton (11)
Horringer Court Middle School, Bury St Edmunds

 132

Help For Heroes

Could it be, that the heroes we see,
Lose their lives, as though stabbed with knives?
They need help our heroes do.

They push themselves to the very limit,
Soldiers dying every minute, leaving family and friends behind,
They need help our heroes do.

Blood running cold, panic is spread,
As bodies are quite often found dead,
They need help our heroes do.

Broken bones, missing limbs and death,
There is no worse fate than death.
They need help our heroes do.

So why don't we help them as much as we can,
Like eliminating the Taliban,
Raising money, they seriously need our help,
Our heroes do.
They help us, let's help them.

Nicky Jeffs (11)
Horringer Court Middle School, Bury St Edmunds

What Is The Earth?

The Earth is a marble, revolving all year round.
The Earth is a star, glistening and when the sunrays hit it,
You can see it from a million miles away,
Like a gorgeous city view.
The Earth is a wraith floating helplessly in a dusky graveyard.
The Earth is a child, looked after by its loving mother, the sun.
The Earth is asleep, awaking only to the beep of cars
And the chatter of people.
The Earth is a happy place to be.

The Earth, we feel safe.

Nikki Jefferson (11)
Horringer Court Middle School, Bury St Edmunds

133

Haiti

The devastation that it's caused.
The lives that have been stopped, like the telly has been paused.
They cry so much for the sake of name,
They are hurt but who's to blame?
It's not their fault, they're just the poor,
All they need is a simple cure.
All they need is a loving home,
Not to be scared and all alone.
Many people's lives are a wreck,
Living on the streets or under a boat's deck.
Under the bricks and rubble is where most people are,
They're up there, each and every star.
Most of them have already lost their lives,
The Devil has now got his prize.
Now Haiti struggles to move on,
Because most of its citizens have gone,
Lives will get better over time,
But not everything will be fine.

Jessica Jarratt, Haley Jefferson & Nikki Jefferson (11)
Horringer Court Middle School, Bury St Edmunds

My Dog Joe

My dog Joe loves cheese,
He had a disgusting taste but loves mushy peas,
When he goes round my nan's he has lots of cups of teas,
That's my weird dog Joe.

He eats the daffodils in the spring,
And he goes wrestling in the ring
And he loves ringing doorbells *'ding!'*
That's my weird dog Joe.

Down the park he runs,
While popping down to the bakery to buy some buns,
While he puts a lot of weight on then he weighs tons,
That's my weird dog Joe.

My dog is turning old,
But he will always stand out bold,
When he's bad he gets left out in the cold
And that's my loving weird dog Joe.

Emma Bradley (12)
Horringer Court Middle School, Bury St Edmunds

Heroes Of The World

They lose their lives
Carrying knives
We call it Hell
Next thing you know the bells are ringing
More of them join
But they don't get coins
We could help
Raising money
Roadside bombs
Full of fear
Scream and shout
Behind and rear
No going back, now can't get out
So come on, let's help.

Becky Mose (11)
Horringer Court Middle School, Bury St Edmunds

The Astronomer

A frail ageing man sat on a chair,
Pensive, reflecting, lost in time,
The intricate constellations,
It all started as a dream

A young boy
With a small telescope on a stand,
Children spent their time playing in the sun
But he spent his time gazing at the night's sky.

He beams intoxicated with the abyss
The appealing concept was simple
Space was so vast, yet so unknown,
Phenomena relied heavily on luck.

At a point during adulthood he was isolated,
Transfixed, consumed by his passion,
Complex notations filled his room,
Silence . . . gaze . . . scribble . . . focus.

The Astronomer returned to reality
His finger rotated the focuses,
His eyes were bloodshot,
Stubble mounted on his wrinkled skin.

The time of wild youth had passed,
Constellations . . . Nebulae . . . meant nothing,
All the hard work and devotion,
Lonely, helpless and stooped.

Leo's sharp claw faltered,
Taurus blinded by rage,
Aquarius followed the currents,
None could dispel his fate

And the end was here,
The notes were ripped,
The telescope was broken
The pencil had snapped.

Darren Kappala-Ramsamy
Ipswich School, Ipswich

137

The Memory Box

On an old rusty bench,
Tucked up in London, she sits
Wearing an old raincoat
Dressed in traveller's kit

As she cries, tears flow into cracks in her skin
Though, no one sees
Passers-by look away. They are closed
Homeless, one of life's losers, they must think
While her old lonely body silently pleads for company,
                                    Acknowledgement

Her mind is elsewhere, bursting at the brink.
She sees not what's in front of her, but the past
Precious memories, enjoyable times
Yet she weeps, she mourns for her happiness
Her hand creeps inside her withered pocket
Concealed within it, a treasured locket
A ticket to another world,
Another lifetime lived decades ago
By a different girl.

For this girl dances till midnight
Wears dresses and a smile
Holding life with high regard all the while
Her mind unleashes a whirlwind of the past
Beautiful holidays, swimming in English seas
Strawberry picking for summer teas
The birth of a child so helpless and small
Meeting Prince Charming at the ball

Time, moments flicker before her
Slowly she closes her eyes
Truly destined for another world . . .

Emma Knights (13)
Ipswich School, Ipswich

138

The Life Of An Oak Tree

The dark earth breaks and shatters,
Upwards and outwards,
As the light green shoots reach desperately
For the glorious morning air

The new child of the forest
Gently brushes away
The old dead leaves that litter
The home of its mighty family

It crawls out slowly,
Ever so slowly
From its secret cave
And climbs so tentatively up towards the heavens

A sibling slowly rises at its side
But it's too late for some
Those who nature has chosen to starve
And fall back downwards in death

Its confidence grows as it nears its goal
Its one true parent ever closer
It shall never reach the flaming orb
But still it climbs ever slowly through the air

It drinks and drinks of its true parents' food,
The sweet golden nectar
That fills up the clearings with joyous music
And dances across the forest sky

Its delicate skin hardens to roughness
Leaves and branches burst from its side
And on them begin to grow new sparks of life
To take over from it when its time finally arrives.

James Norrington Hughes-Stanton (16)
Ipswich School, Ipswich

139

Dusty Pup

The leather is cracked and faded,
His chair
Thick curtains obstruct the rays of dusk,
The television crackles - he remembers,
The crackle of gun embers.

Resounding through young ears,
Mud slimes up his polished boots,
And the sky above is dark,
A young girl's face fades to smoke,
From naivety's dream woke.

Salty blood pours from chapped lips,
Eluded by dreams of glory,
But do we remember him now?
Young and old.
Warm and cold.

Plucked out until all that
Remains are the weak frail feathers,
He left his hope of the fields,
Like an empty walnut,
Left in a rut.

The prime of his life taken away,
By selfish politics.
And in return he now gets
A 10 to 3 slot
At a local corner shop.

Emily Jeffery (14)
Ipswich School, Ipswich

140

The Misunderstood

As the sun over the hill pries,
You prepare for yet more lies,
Allegations and humiliation,
All while we work for you.

In a room in which we gather,
Over a decision we all do dither,
The most despised
Scapegoats from men,
All in our jobs for you.

Sitting with our Fair Trade coffee,
Discussing different types of toffee,
We confer and discuss
The best kind of bus,
Even though we have no clue.

People often come to complain,
About our handling of snow and rain,
Late reactions,
No capital investment,
Disappointment spreads like a plague again.

The end of the day, we've done our job,
Now home for corn on the cob.
We may have two homes or more,
But such rife contention?
We're not so different, they, and us.

James Holmes (14)
Ipswich School, Ipswich

141

Untitled

The moon gleams on dark water with all its might,
It gives light that is astonishingly bright,
Yet it is not its own, you see,
As it comes from the sun, which shines beautifully.

The water ebbs and flows,
It almost glows,
The moon is reflected more than one time, on more than one lake
It seems so fake.

The waters shine
It is really divine,
The moon reflects like a mirror,
It looks like it's getting nearer.

The moon so close,
It looks like it is in a pose,
It has perfectly neat lines,
Each night it shows different signs.

The trees surrounding are dark,
There is a spark,
The night sky so black,
It looks like if you touch it, it would crack.

Pip Boocock (13)
Ipswich School, Ipswich

142

Soldier, Soldier

Yes, I am a soldier,
Well it started as a dream,
I wanted to be one of those respected men,
Yet I am lost within this world,
I took a job as a street ranger, yet in my mind I knew I was wrong.
Every night I would battle in my sleep, trying to win the battle in
my dream.
My eyes would be wide open in the day, coming to terms with not
getting a job,
Walking down an abandoned alleyway, I know I am a losing soldier,
Lost in the muddy, horrific battlefield, our world.
I keep on trying to understand my place in this battlefield,
I am being targeting, yet I am a threat to this world,
Remember this lost soldier, young, alone, already forgotten,
I am a lost soldier, just a mist in the eyes of many.
Please come and find this lost, *lost* soldier,
Welcome me to a neighbourhood where I can win the battle in
my dream.
And now my mind is rested, I have won the battle in my mind.
I have been to war.

Georgina Everett-Beecham
Ipswich School, Ipswich

Once The Snow Is Gone

An icy white blanket that once covered the world,
The intricate dainty flakes that once quickly twirled,
Mixed emotions caused from just ice and bitter cold,
Once melted: woe, joy and a story to be told.

As the bright sun strongly appears,
Children's joyful faces disappear,
The frosty white begins to retreat,
As it turns to water from the heat.

The fresh spring grass sneaks through,
Looking dirtier than usual too,
Only in comparison to the perfect white,
That wreaked havoc with all its might.

Once the perfect white has run away,
And the Arctic cold is at bay,
The road no longer lethal,
We wish for the return of the white evil!

Tabitha Maserr-Clarke
Ipswich School, Ipswich

After The Snow

Frozen ice
Suddenly still
But you pay the price
When you slide down the hill.

Everything glitters in the sunlight
A rainbow of snow across the land
So cold, yet it is so bright
You wear gloves and get a tan.

Slipping and sliding
As the snowmen take over
Kids playing snowball, are hiding
While others run and duck for cover.

The weather was having a race
The spring has won
All clouds vanish without a trace
I know the snow will be back before long.

Courtney Witter (13)
Ipswich School, Ipswich

Forever

A pale sunset
Laid its head on the water's wall
So how could I forget
The time I thought I had it all

The evening sky
Extinguished its light for the night
So how can I but try
To forget when we would just fight

The stone cold sand
Settles down when the day is done
So how can I demand
We stay like this, for you'll have won

I'll say goodbye,
This time I mean it forever
Try your best not to cry
We weren't meant to be together.

Megan Whincop (15)
Kesgrave High School, Kesgrave

It (V 2 0)

Past, present, future,
It is there,
The voice,
It is there.

Everything and
       Nothing

The sound of the crashing waves.
The softness of a lover's touch.
The heat off the street,
The music that makes you move.

Everything and
       Nothing

Silent, shifting, changing,
It is always there.
I know what it is.
I bet you do.

The voice
It is . . .
There
It is . . .

The sound of a baby's first cry,
The sigh of a forest as,
It finally breathes spring air.
The beat, the rhythm that is always there.
Keeps you going.
Past, present, future.
Feel it, know it, love it.
You know what it is.
Just think.

Rebecca Brown (16)
Kingham Hill School, Chipping Norton

147

To Be A Memory

I won't, I won't
I will not fade
From other's memories
I will not let
Myself be lost
I won't conform to be
Another one,
A memory
A person lost in time
I'll work to make
My memory
Solidified in rhyme.

Or else I'll try
Some other way
To set myself in stone
I'll make it big
I'll do it great
To make my presence known
I'll make sure that
No one forgets
I won't fade to the dark
Inside your hearts,
Your memories
I'll strive to make my mark.

Jacob Annis (16)
Kingham Hill School, Chipping Norton

Dancing Dream

Twirling tremendously, right across the stage
Leaping in their leotards, red, gold and beige
Doing wonderful kicks, high in the air
With their pink laced ballet shoes
And matching ribbon in their hair

Bending from second position, into plea
Waving yellow ballet sticks, like a golden sunray
Tension in the audience, nobody knows
Will they jump, leap, twirl or go up on their toes?

It looks nice to be a ballerina
Dancing with glee
But they are them
And I am me.

Lucy Alldis-Clark (11)
Larkmead School, Abingdon

Time, Time, Time, Time

Handle time with care,
It's always ticking away.
Try and keep it close.
Time, time, time, time.
New beginning of a lifetime.
Believe, imagine, with hope,
What could happen in time?
A friend, an enemy,
A helping hand.
You never know what time could bring,
So keep it close because you never know what's going to
Happen next.

Emelia Bell (12)
Lincroft School, Oakley

149

The Finish

Sunrise, sunset,
Sunrise, sunset,
Each day older,
Each day closer,
Closer to the finish line,
Closer to the end of time,
End of times of friendship, fun,
Love, hate, sadness, I am done,
But isn't it the human way,
Be born, then live and die someday,
See, the journey is not done,
I must finish what's begun.
Finish, finish, but what then?
Do I disappear into thin air?
We don't know, we never will,
But let's be optimistic still,
Maybe another journey starts.
I don't know, just ask the stars.
But the stars remain silent, they know,
Time will soon burn out their glow,
All we can do is hope and pray,
That we'll live forever after that day.

Gabriela Gurycz (12)
Lincroft School, Oakley

New Beginning

Through the ash and decay, a new seed is born,
Through life, trials will tear you down and beat you.
But you can change all of the pain and scorn,
Into something fresh and something new.

You hold the key to opening up your own life,
It's your choice to determine which path you walk.
Walk the road carrying a gun or a knife,
Or open your mouth and start to talk.

It's your own choice, it's your own destiny,
To dance in fields of green while the fires blaze.
To ride the wind and soar the sky, free.
Wake in the morning and watch the cattle graze.

Rush to the windows and taste the first snow,
Sway with the ocean and sail to the moon.
Plan a trip to rival travellers, and then just go,
Long to see a love and hope that it's soon.

Race your heart to the beat of the music,
Jump free and never feel a touch of the ground.
Live a life of nectar and ripe fruit to pick,
Listen to owls and return their sound.

Float across the sky like a star burning bright,
Bargain with nature so you never get old.
Marvel at the senses of touch and sight,
So many stories that you'll live to be told.

Just enjoy the free existence of a single day,
Don't hold back, every moment is free.
Don't waste a second, that's the price you pay,
It happens to all and right now, it's happening to me.

Callum Haskins (17)
North Herts College, Stevenage

151

Of Fire And Wind

Of fire and wind I am silent,
I would spread my wings if these bars did not press so tight,
And fly to ascending heavens of tribulation,
Where I may find peace,
Alas,
I have no peace,
I have no heaven,
No wings,
Nothing but these bars, and the fire and the wind
And if I may shout above them with all might,
My voice is still silent,
Carried only upon the wind,
And lost to the fire.

I have built a dam,
With walls impassable,
Which tower over,
To block my view,
And cordon off the corners of my mind,
To push back the waters of my past,
But all things must come to an end.
And when I had forgotten what the waters hold,
And lost why I must have a wall,
I tore you down,
And came to regret it,
What a foolish act.
With endless waves of time gone by,
I now wash myself in stagnant memories,
The tidal thoughts,
Which are forced to repeat their acts.

Andrew Dilley (18)
North Herts College, Stevenage

152

The Music

As I pick up my guitar
My aching fingers regain feeling
Lifted by a new-found energy
I start to strum
Effortlessly playing
With a new extension of my body
All worries gone from the world
Washed away by my gentle music
I feel at ease
At peace with the world
I become one with the music.

Jake Perry (18)
North Herts College, Stevenage

The Beat

The beat goes on
Never stopping
Never hesitating
Or even pausing
One beat after another
And on and on and on
But wait!
The beat is different.
It does not feel normal.
The beat is stopping
It is not regular
It is slowing
The beat is dying
It *stopped!*

William Hempstead (11)
Parkside Federation, Cambridge

153

The Bunker

A massed section of concrete on all sides,
That to some used to be a danger,
But to others a home, a sanctuary and a life-saver.
Used to stand strong in a landscape and flaunt its power,
For what they thought would be centuries.

Though, now it stands as a meagre tourist attraction
And as the generations pass, it slowly decays to a picture in a
text book.
With few coming to pay their respects and many more coming
To violate it with their vulgar forms of artwork; defacing the
Once-strong frontier of defence.

It shows no sign of immorality now,
As the trees and plants slowly take back what is rightfully theirs.
The dark green moss slowly inhabits the soldiers' living quarters,
And the army of ferns takes their shady home next to a
gun emplacement.
The present coming together with the future, for the purpose of
Destroying the past; as nature unknowingly eradicates
human construction.

The path in front takes the thousands walking straight past each day
And when someone gets a glimpse they do not see a monument
Anymore, but a corroding hideous manmade thing.

The future looks bleak for this little piece of history.
As it will slowly be taken back and destroyed by the advancing
eco-system.
Maybe before that, it will be used as a home, either for creatures
Or the people our society casts out as dirt.
But it is always the same: man destroying but nature always
Prevailing, it works together as one force but we work as many.

The only thing we know for certain is that this little piece of history
shall be lost.
In what way we do not know, but in the end we shall lose it from
our memory.

Kim Michael Sorensen (15)
Parkside Federation, Cambridge

154

Living, Not Dreaming

Sitting, lying, thinking, wondering,
Everything around so uninspiring,
I'm dreaming of living, I long for creativity.

A cacophony of rainbow swirls,
All jostling for attention.
Uncharted territory, a kaleidoscope world
Without rules, aims or intention.

An explosion of light and sound,
Bright then shadow, seeing and feeling,
I'll be inundated with things to be found,
There'll be no waiting, just believing.

I want so many experiences,
Haunting melodies, a flash of light
A new scent pricking at my nostrils
With a sense that everything is right.

I'll escape from walls, one shade of grey,
So cold, dank and depressing.
No more rooms that act as prison cells,
Built for quelling and oppressing.

And it will be real,
I can't live life to the full,
With half the fat skimmed off,
And stuck inside a bottle.

I'm beginning to ebb away, in here,
Dreaming of living,
So many new concepts,
Almost too much to bear.

But one day I'll escape
From this barren desolate landscape,
Then I'll be living not dreaming!

Camilla King (12)
Parkside Federation, Cambridge

155

I Saw Love

At the start of the hill, at the end of the silent cliff
Where the sun does shine, where the wind does blow
There, upon the edge of the world
At the beginning and end of love
There I looked upon the world in its wonder
There I pondered and wondered and remembered.

To once when I was on top of a hillock
Where I looked
To the sea loving the land
And I wondered
Was it the land loving the sea?
And as I stood there, I remembered

To once when I crouched alongside a riverbank
Where the river was calling me
Or was it me
Calling the river?
And as I crouched, I wondered
What was to come?

Later
I fell, fell, fell
From the top of a mountain
Where death was calling me
Or was it me calling death?
And I saw

I saw how to be thankful and to forgive
I saw how to open my eyes
And as I stood on that lonely hill at the edge of the silent cliff
I saw light
Working with darkness
I saw love.

Aneurin Quinn Evans (12)
Parkside Federation, Cambridge

156

Captain Patel's Trunk
(Inspired by 'Magic Box' by Kit Wright)

I will put in my trunk . . .
The first time I saw the smile of my mother and father,
The warmth I felt when I sat on my grandad's lap,
The tingling feeling I had when my grandma first hugged me.

I will put in my trunk . . .
The day I said my first word,
The love I feel towards my mother when she touches me,
The time I wore my first dress, the feeling of the silk touching my skin.

I will put in my trunk . . .
The flight that I took to India when I was six,
The time when I first put my foot on Portuguese Land,
The day I saw Mickey Mouse and Minnie in their house
inside Disneyland.

I will put in my trunk . . .
The trip when my mother and I went to Hunstanton
The last time I saw the house I was born in and spent eight years in
Three wishes spoken in Swahili.

My trunk is fashioned from amethyst, ruby and pearls.
Its hinges are the wings of fairies.
The corners are different worlds.
The lid is a magical land full of forests and flowers.

I shall play in my box
With an imaginary friend.
I shall go to the corner of the trunk
To the tower of Pisa in Italy.
I will take my imaginary friend and
Explore the magical land on the lid.

Janki Patel (12)
Parkside Federation, Cambridge

Heroes

When I am old and looking back
Who will the heroes be?
What deeds will they have done?
Because one of them will be me

Will there be Spider-Man
Swinging in the air?
Or will there be Superman
Cutting his big hair?

When I was five and had nothing to do
I was really getting bored
So I tied my cape and then I escaped
With my big golden sword.

My Nintendo Wii was really fun
And I was playing 'Sonic Unleashed'
And the end of level there was a bonus stage
Where you get to be a beast

My favourite hero is Sonic the Hedgehog
Because I like his speed
He's normally blue because he's very fast
And I wanna be fast too.

When I am old and looking back
Who will the heroes be?
What deeds will they have done?
Because one of them will be me.

Because I'm just a student
And I get so bored in school
I'll call my favourite superheroes
So people will think I'm cool!

Wahidur Rahman (11)
Parkside Federation, Cambridge

158

The Time Puddle

Setting slowly, the sun descended the amber sky.
I walk through the park and I wonder: why?
Why doesn't anyone think I'm interesting?
I suppose it's because I haven't done anything.
Nothing exciting after all my ten years,
But then I see something that makes the fogs clear.
I come across a puddle, and dip in my toe,
And what happened next, you probably know.
In I fell, down, down, down,
And I found myself in a Victorian town,
I stayed stuck for about an hour
Before I realised I had a special power,
When I clicked my fingers, and shouted out 'Puddle',
I could go anywhere, without a muddle.
'Puddle', the dinosaurs, 'Puddle', the war,
I knew this would never become a bore,
The Romans, the Stone Age, The Blitz, 'This is mad!'
I could witness the birth of my mum and dad!
After I'd been to the year 3002,
I wondered next, what should I do?
These places were all crammed full of facts,
But now I really just wanted to go back,
I tried shouting, 'Puddle,' and imagined my street,
And found myself suddenly whisked off my feet.
I was finally back and very pleased,
Of the adventure that I had achieved.
I went to my friends and then I called out,
'Listen to me, for I've been about!'
Then I realised with a sense of fear,
They didn't care if I'd been far or near.

Isabel Tucker Brown (13)
Parkside Federation, Cambridge

The Four Seasons

Spring
Frost clearing
Birds singing
Little green stalks coming out of the soil.

It is a time for rebirth
It is a time to forgive sins.

Summer
Leaves shine green,
Flowers bloom,
Beaches are packed with joyful families.

It is a time for rejoicing
It is a time for happiness.

Autumn
Leaves browning
Trees bear fruits
Animals hibernate to get away from the cold.

It is a time for reflection
It is a time for falling apart.

Winter
Trees bare,
Breath mists
Snow glistens, white and cold.

It is a time for death,
It is a time for loss.

However, as snowdrops poke their heads through the frost,
Spring comes again.

Eve Caroe (12)
Parkside Federation, Cambridge

160

Betraying Love And Flaming Hearts

The pain of losing you
Is more than I thought
Recovering from this s**t
Just can't be taught.

I thought you cared
Oh how I was wrong
You had a place in my heart
I guess you didn't belong

I could be by your side
For years if you needed me
But you plunged a knife into my heart
Just with the words you wickedly threw at me

You let little stories
Get in the way
Of what we were
You changed through the day

I just can't help it
I don't want to resent you but I do
I want you to be by me
We could be 'me and you'

Death and love
Come hand in hand
Without one there's the other
You kicked me from this Promised Land.

Michael Tusnia (14)
Parkside Federation, Cambridge

Unrequited Adulation

You are hopeful to enrapture her, The One.
The One that resonates with happiness,
The One that satiates with euphoria,
The One of unparalleled attractiveness.

You strive to seize her benevolent affection,
But she merely panders to your passion.
A disposable minion under casual control,
Your gullible heart starts to wearily blacken.

You believe your love could help her blossom,
Yet, she evades eager eyes with gentle grace,
To admire, as you, in disheartened loneliness,
At some fortunate other's neglecting face.

Nothing can you do, nothing can you say,
She's oblivious to your 'too loyal' stare.
However, she still fulfils you with optimism,
Even when her rejection is bitter to bear.

We lust for possessions we cannot own.
A perpetual cycle of aching pains,
Of unanswered lovers who remain loveless
And the loved ones, who love in vain.

After, our shattered hope begins to dissipate
And we descend to the depths of grief and affliction.
Although, we pray one day we'll emerge, repaired,
To find someone else who yearns for mutual affection.

Max Tomlinson (14)
Parkside Federation, Cambridge

162

Lost Inside

Once I got lost in my bedroom
It had nothing to do with a map.
The place where I go and have dream time
The place where I go take a nap,
Was gone and instead there before me,
Were acres and acres of cloud.
The Goggles were singing quite surely
The Finglewops really were loud.

A Flobswob was smiling right at me
His teeth all askew in his mouth
He pointed towards a great building
He seemed to be saying 'Go South.'
So I wandered the route he had told me,
To a river of flaxen hair,
And laughed at a red Cock-a-poodle
Who was holding hands with a bear.

The book that I shut was a big one
All blue and gold leather so smart,
I was sitting at home in my bedroom
Whilst my brothers played 'Mario Kart'.
I thought, as I sat on my soft chair
It must be nearly time for some brunch,
Or perhaps I'd been reading so long now
That it was nearly time for my lunch.

Aphra Hiscock (11)
Parkside Federation, Cambridge

163

The Only Immortal

It stalks in the night to feed
To feed on the fear it breeds
It breeds in every corner
Every corner of every house
In every house a child wishes for the sun
The sun can banish it
Banish it but only for twelve
For twelve, the other twelve, it roams
It roams not only on Earth
On Earth it is feared
It is feared elsewhere too
Other planets,
Other worlds
Other galaxies
It is feared even by the stars
The stars can die but it can't
It won't
It won't for knowledge that
One day
It will rule
Because darkness
Is
The only immortal.

Daniel Moore (13)
Parkside Federation, Cambridge

164

Moo

In a field there were cows all stood in the mud,
When an elderly brown one looked up from the cud,
It addressed its fellows in a polite way:
'Have you heard the news today?'
'Yes,' came the answer from a bull near the field,
'The parcel of victory is surely sealed.'
Then a large cow proclaimed from its place near the fence:
'Come over here and listen hence.
I have some much more exciting news.'
The comment was met with excited 'oohs',
'I've come up with a brilliant algebra sum.
I made it up yesterday, purely for fun.'
Now the cow was about to launch into a description,
Full of symbols, long numbers and the force of friction,
But before she could say any more than a word,
'Have you read Shakespeare?'' asked the boss of the herd,
But then a small cow said, 'We do this every day.'
So they went back to grass in their herbivore way.

Now a man called Ben was present for all of this talk,
It had been stuffy at home so he'd gone for a walk,
He'd been near to the field and near the cows too,
Yet the only sound he heard . . . was moo.

Amy Packwood (11)
Parkside Federation, Cambridge

Leaving

You think it would be better
Starting a new life, a quieter
Neighbourhood, no guns,
No knives.

That's what your dreams
Are about, to just move away
But when you're down, you'd
Wished you had stayed.

You think it's just a laugh
But you're not dreaming no more
A completely different house
With a new-coloured door.

You're used to your stuff
Being in the right place,
You're so used to seeing
The same pretty faces.

But that's all changed
Time for a fresh start
But my sister, my mum
Will always stay in my heart.

Tianna Mason (13)
Parkside Federation, Cambridge

166

Death

It isn't a word,
It's a feeling.
A passage of time for all,
Cutting like a dagger,
Through hearts and souls,
A wound so deep a tremendous fall,
Only love can heal it,
Love and time,
Love and time beat,
Death.

Hope Shaw (13)
Parkside Federation, Cambridge

167

Domestic Violence

For how long will I grieve?
My happiness slowly fades like colour
I can't accommodate all your wishes
Mind you! Flexibility is for business, not me!

I feel intrinsically small around you
Is this love I was longing for? My dear husband
Always on the look out for my mistakes
Too ignorant of my achievements
If you sold me, I guess it would be for nothing.

I thought slavery vanished years ago
I rummage for solutions to my suffering
But alas, instead of issues I get tissues
Daily I mourn and wish for a better tomorrow

I feel obliged to call myself 'liar'
Because I smile only to please you, what a deceiving gesture!
I agree to satisfy you . . . nothing else.
Always afraid of upsetting and losing you
Is this what they call love?

Nothing we do together you appreciate
You dare call me childish! But I am old, old and so tired.
I always sacrifice my happiness for your pleasure

Society has completely forgotten about domestic violence
Children ought to be a source of happiness, so why shatter
their dreams?
Children are future foundations but we destroy this base
Yet we cry for a better society!

Nicholas Mushaike (17)
Pestalozzi International Village, Battle

168

Freedom Fight

I wonder what crimes I committed,
To have never seen my land.
I wonder what lady fate has decided,
For all the unborn, mute Tibetans.

For an innocent child to be born without
A land to call his own,
As a refugee what future,
To be ever labelled with an R?

People say 'It needs a fight -
For helping you feel free.'
But can the fact that you did fight
Satisfy the pain?

For the R stays branded deep and clear
And nothing is achieved,
Is it worth the freedom fight
When it does not set you free?

I feel the pain inside my heart,
For a land that is taken for dead.
What is it like to hold your head high?
What is it to be free?

Is it worth all the pain, the suffering, the blood?
It is frightening, the fight to be free.

But I will suffer the pain that comes with an R.
For my sons, for a future, for a Free Tibet.

Tenzin Tenpa (17)
Pestalozzi International Village, Battle

169

Cries Of A Baby

Don't cry, don't cry,
For there is no mother left here to hug you

It was my next-door neighbour yesterday
It is my closest cousin today,
And if tomorrow comes,
I cannot discount myself.

Ladies and Gentlemen,

A gathering is incomplete
Without a loss to AIDS

It is a pity to know that all who know
The dangers of HIV
Have yet to follow what they preach
And be the saints of day and night

During the day they preach and pray
And yet by night . . .
For *if the night turned into day,*
A lot of people would run away.

But AIDS provides nowhere to run
And the killer is here to stay
And so who will care for the poor child
When Mother and Father ail?

I can hear the cry of the poor child and I can also hear a voice,
The shaky song of a lullaby from a grandmother singing for hope.

Nickolet Ncube (18)
Pestalozzi International Village, Battle

170

The Ode To Freedom

Pushed to the ground by your burdens,
My shoulders are heavy laden,
Caged by tradition and fear,
Death of good is far and near.

We are chained by war and prejudice,
Instead of a brother you see a race,
And your shallowness blinds you to eternal grace,
And you may not remember this face.

But you will remember every word,
And you will put away your sword,
For I am the voice of your dream,
A fountain of thoughts that flow as a stream.

I am every immortal man, who in history came,
And on whose brow all men inscribe their name,

I will march for your freedom,
I will fight the oppressor in you,

I will turn this Earth into your home,
And I will liberate you,

I will protect you,
I will affect you,

Giants will look up to me,
And your memories will grant me immortality.

Ruth Mwangase (18)
Pestalozzi International Village, Battle

171

The Future Is In Our Hands

The future of our land
Has always sat in the human hand
From Stone Age to Iron Age
Iron Age to the modern day

Let's bring pollution to an end
If we have the will to mend
Let's stop the blackening of our skies
Global warming is in our eyes

Fossils fuels pollute everywhere
And we cannot deny, we are aware
The air we breathe will kill
If we continue to let the gases spill

We need an energy solution
To end such widespread, dark pollution

Let's take care not to damage our health
As we follow the quest for wealth
Let us stop the pollution today
To reduce the price we are to pay

The ozone layer cannot be replaced
Beware! The Earth may be defaced.
Our hands can make, and shape and mould,
Let us forge a future bright and bold.

Tongai Ndlovu (18)
Pestalozzi International Village, Battle

172

A Life Dilemma

What is life?
Someone asked me
And I could not help my tears
Thinking, *why are they asking me?*

Then,

I thought and thought until
I met an old friend.
He tried his hardest to console
And elaborate -

Life is most wonderful and
So beautiful you see . . .
But I showed him the begging man
And his bare feet on the road.

I heard many more philosophise,
Say *Life is the dew on a rosy cheek,*
But those who quote had not the cost
Of a Life now lost to me, the son.

I thought of lovely Mother and thought
Of all the quotes
And thought of my dilemma
For living in this life.

Pravin Kamble (17)
Pestalozzi International Village, Battle

173

Miracle

The sun was not yet risen,
The ground was fresh with dew,
My heart was pounding in a rhythm,
Which set my stride length true.

He said I should not race,
My owner forced me to,
But now my heart was on the case,
I knew what I had to do.

The gun went with a bang,
My ears pricked with shock,
Upon my back he hung,
His legs in my side like a lock.

I could see my legs beneath me,
My hind was brushed with fear,
My life was fading easily,
As the ground started to disappear.

I tumbled with the pain,
In a forward somersault.
The mud was matted in my mane,
As I tried to get up and bolt.

The vet examined my broken bone,
He shook his head and sighed,
Low and sorrowful was his tone,
'I am sorry but I have tried.'

'No,' he shouted in his sorrow.
'Put him down, you shall not,
Any money, I will borrow.
I will not see him shot!'

So in a lorry, homeward bound,
My weight within a sling,
Next, my stable, safe and sound,
He could not help but sing.

The next few weeks were nothing but
Recovery road for me,
But now the door was no longer shut,
At last, at last I was free.

I began to walk and then to trot,
Building up to something faster.
Round and round that tiring plot,
But I owed it to my master.

My master whispered in my ear
'I have taken you slow and steady,
You need not worry about your fear,
For I think that you are ready.'

The race day approached so fast, so fast,
In the lorry I found myself once more,
Could I win, like the times gone past?
Yes I could win, and of that I was sure.

The sun was not yet risen,
The ground was fresh with dew,
My heart was pounding in a rhythm,
Which set my stride length true.

Katie Kennett (12)
Rye St Antony School, Oxford

175

The Ballad Of Madeleine McCann

It was a perfect holiday
The family was happy together.
Laughing and playing all day long
They thought it would last
Forever.

On one fateful evening of May
As the children went to sleep.
The parents left them all alone,
As the babysitter's fee was too steep.

While having dinner
Someone noticed a man,
Carrying a child down the road
Who then drove off in a van.

An hour went by
And the mother returned
To check on her sleeping angels,
Hoping to find them undisturbed.

She spots the two babies
Lying quietly in their cot.
But where did Madeleine go?
Her bed screams emptiness and loss.

The mother shrieks and screams
From room to room she runs
Then out to the empty street she flees
Praying loudly, 'God, help us!'

'Madeleine's gone!
They've taken her!'
She keeps on repeating it endlessly:
'They've taken her!'

The police arrive,
Photographs appear
The questioning is underway
Meanwhile, all traces disappear.

They have searched for her everywhere
From early morning till late at night
For weeks on end without fail
They've never given up the fight.

The agony was killing them
Her parents felt so responsible.
Why, oh why did they leave them alone?
Their act is unforgivable.

Sorrowful years flew by
And still many pray,
For Madeleine to be found,
The search still continues today.

Dorothy Papp (12)
Rye St Antony School, Oxford

A Sonnet For Zac Efron

Oh, I could sit all day staring at you,
And your beautiful, starry, big, blue eyes,
I know that my love for you will be as true,
Like the sun coming up in the warm sky,

Oh how much I love your perfect physique,
Smooth and tanned with a six-pack to die for,
Your Hollywood smile has such a mystique,
I had never seen anyone like you before.

When you flick your brown, wavy, swishy hair
You win my heart over again and again
Every time I see you on my wide screen
You look so amazing it hurts my brain.

Oh, damn! I wish that I could resist you.
It's all fantasy, but will never come true.

Lucy Warde-Aldam (14)
Rye St Antony School, Oxford

177

A Girl In Haiti

In the islands of the Caribbean
Lies a beautiful sparkling place
An island named Haiti
Where a frown falls on many a face

Amongst it all are the people
Scattered all along the island
Troubled by crime and poverty
It seems God they have not found

Tremors running through the earth
People screaming everywhere
The ground is shaking endlessly
The sheer impact comes out of nowhere

Screams of pain and helplessness
Uncontrollable forces of devastation
All over the shouts of wounded people
Everybody fearing depravation

Entire buildings crumble into dust
With people trapped beneath
With no food or water to help them live
Death soon became a thief

In the middle of all this
A young girl named Marie
Trapped in the shadows
With the bodies of her beloved family

Protected by the old wooden table
Climbing out of the wreckage she survives
Everything and everybody lost in the dust
Counting herself lucky to be alive

Stumbling into the light
Afraid, hesitating with tears in her eyes
Not knowing where to go
All senses numbed, no shelter from the cries

Wandering about looking for nothing
Children shouting for Mom but no help was there
Desperation growing in her heart
Eyes burning the scent of death spreading everywhere

Slow, limping, shuffling steps
Powerless, uneven, her walk still lasts
Nothing she remembered, not anything in her mind
Her body trembles - her life flashes past

Her walk coming to a sudden stop
Her blood streaking her face with the taste of tears
Pain striking the back of her head
The end was near - the pain was gone - death so clear.

Valentina Patt (14)
Rye St Antony School, Oxford

If I Was Cornwall Then You Are My Hills

You're a breathtaking gorgeous Cornwall sea
Every time I see you our bright love gains
You go to the lighthouse there I will be
If I was the storm you are my rains

Your rough wavy hair is sandy and blonde
Your sea green eyes came out a starry cave
Every day I am with you our love bonds
If I was the ocean then you're my wave

You're tall as a mast on a painted boat
We lie on the beach as the seagulls cry
Crisps by the rocks on your seaweed green coat
If I was a cloud then you are my sky

I love being with you, the awesome thrills
If I was Cornwall, then you are my hills.

Tilly Rand-Bell (13)
Rye St Antony School, Oxford

179

The Ballad Of Fiona Donnison

At the end of cold January
In a deserted car park
Two children were breathing
The last air in the dark

Fiona Donnison wandered off
To Heathfield police station
With her mud-coloured face
Blabbed out the emotions

She and Paul divorced a week ago
They both knew why, but they had tears
Divorce made her blank minded
That made her kill two dears

In a sports bag, Harry and Elise
Forced in there, by their mother, Fi
Used up all the air in there
Crouching down on their knee

At Lewes Magistrate's court
All her relatives watching her
Fiona was arrested
Needing broken heart cure

She was taken away in the end
'We love you, Fi!' a woman cried
She walked off as stiff as a stick
Policemen at her side

'Lights that shone the brightest in my life'
Paul Donnison states this clearly
This isn't to be done again
It hurts people surely

We must all learn something from this news
Murder does not solve anything
It breaks and aches people's hearts
Just kills and ruins many things

180

At the end of cold January
In a deserted car park
Two children were breathing
The last air in the dark.

Mari Esashi (12)
Rye St Antony School, Oxford

Ryan . . .

The gleaming blue of his unmissable eyes,
His muscular figure waiting for me,
The feather-like strands lay soft on his head,
His smooth hands ran easily over me.

No earthly sounds rolled off his perfect tongue,
Only those from Heaven excited him,
The ripples of muscles as he laughed,
Holding me close as his scent circles me.

He floats across the brightly coloured room,
As our eyes met I blush, then we are alone,
All the music fades into the background,
The gap slowly closed between our bodies.

You are my star in the empty night sky,
My heart is yours after our love full life.

Daisy Howard (14)
Rye St Antony School, Oxford

The Ballad Of Mo Mowlem

On the 18th of September
In 1949,
A very precious lady
Was born into our time.

Her life was very eventful,
She married her boy Jon.
Mo smoked and her hands did shake,
Soon her life had been and gone.

At the Charing Cross Hospital
In 1997,
Her tumour was diagnosed,
It sent her up to Heaven.

Average survival, 2/3 years.
Left frontal lobe of brain
Cancerous or malignant.
Dr Glazer was his name.

Weight gain, hair loss, sickness, balance,
Just to climb the stair.
These were her many problems,
The sight was hard to bear.

She had to tell her busy boss.
The wig: 'Such a bother',
She took it off at work.
Tony Blair, her employer.

4th of September 2000
Announced retirement.
In 2001,
Carry on: she couldn't.

Very sadly she fell over,
Just with that one dive,
She never woke up
Just aged 55.

Rose Kirtley (12)
Rye St Antony School, Oxford

182

A Game Fit For A King

A beautiful game that's fit for a king,
Smooth silk racquets made out of solid gold,
Smash it, over it goes, over the net,
All other games just leave me so stone-cold.

The crowd so quiet, not a whisper about,
The ball gets toss'd in the air . . . and then smash,
The crowd bellows with excitement and cheers,
The ball hits the ground with a terrible crash.

The players all dressed in ice-cold soft white,
With raindrops of sweat, drip-dropping off their chins,
Their bodies bound in stiff, white sticky tape,
And bruises and cuts all up to their shins.

The thumps in their heads, they serve the last shot,
To lose in this game, would make them distraught.

Georgie Plunket (13)
Rye St Antony School, Oxford

Time

Summer freezes into winter
Baby grows into a man
Scarlet sun descends
Yellow sun rises
So quickly
Passes
Time
But
That time
Is wasted
Effortlessly
Golden hours become
Foolishly empty seconds
And so our time is meaningless.

Sophie Platt (12)
Rye St Antony School, Oxford

183

It's In!

The crowd is deathly quiet,
They know it's almost over,
Whichever way it goes,
I'm sure they'll be a riot.

I take a few steps back,
The crowd are in disbelief,
How did he not get a red,
For such a blatant hack?

I can see the keeper fretting,
The wall is lining up.
They stare into my eyes,
I feel myself sweating.

I start to begin my run up,
My foot strikes the ball,
It goes over the wall,
In my eyes I see the cup.

It curls towards the far post,
I see it dip and swerve.
The keeper dives gallantly,
But this would've beaten most.

The keeper flicks into the goal
It's in! I've scored the winner!
I've scored an impossible shot!
The stadium erupts as a whole.

I've won us the FA Cup,
I've made Sunderland proud,
This is the best moment in my life
The Black Cats are on the up!

Tom Guntrip (14)
St Birinus' School, Didcot

184

World War I In The Trenches

We all laid there muddy and wet
Wondering if we'd ever succeed
We all laid there, wondering what to do
And if we'd ever exceed.

Then the sergeant blew his whistle
And we prepared for the advance
We checked our rifles and prepared our bombs
We thought we were in a trance.

We ran past the barbed wire
And saw the enemy line.
We raised our weapons, preparing to fire
We thought this was a crime.

The bullets came, the noises deafening
We had very little hope
Our battalion was reduced in seconds
We knew we couldn't cope.

The sergeant shouted to retreat
He knew we'd had enough
We turned our backs on the enemy line
I didn't think it would be this tough.

When I reached the trenches
I quickly dived back in
I wanted to be back home
Away from this awful sin.

Only a few ever returned
I felt like a muddy sack
So I laid down, closed my eyes
And waited for the next attack.

Sam Dent (14)
St Birinus' School, Didcot

Waterfall

Calm waves take me faraway
Life's streams carry me to a new home.
A safe haven far from this place.
I feel no pain but soft words as I am dragged onwards.
The river's waters speak kindly to me in soothing voices
That sing out across my conscience.
Take me further, I see nothing through my blind eyes.
I reach the edge of this world and look down on my next.

The fall is great but I have no fear in my heart.
I fly free through the clouds as the stars pass me by.
What small travellers are we in the days of eternity,
That we gently pass through in our short years.
I know not where I am nor where I will be,
I feel the velvet smoke drift in and out of me
As I channel through this void.

Then I am gone, forever unknown, lost and consumed by the
mists of eternity.
The jaws of isolation swallow me whole and I am trapped in time
once again.
I find myself missing in the colourless nothingness.
I swim down to the surface breaking the realms of impossibility.
I vanish, I disappear.
And I am gone.

Geno Naughton (13)
St Birinus' School, Didcot

Nervous

As the carriage leaves the station
I get a nervous sensation
Because it lacks speed
I can view all the trees
It goes up high
As I get a numb thigh
My legs are shaking
My life is fading
I'm so scared
And not prepared
It does a barrel roll,
Through a giant hole
Speeding very fast
I'm not gonna be last
It arrives at the station
With my nervous sensation.

Joe Tuckwell (14)
St Birinus' School, Didcot

Time

What a horrible year it was this time,
The death and corruption of 2009;
Terrorists committing vast genocide
And politicians with something to hide.
Vast arrays of the old world dead
But let's talk about the future instead.
Now then it is time to pick up my pen
And talk about my aspirations for 2010.
New talent found despite the demise of Simon Cowell
Will have the pendants howl with joy
And the release of the latest shiny toy,
And a lawsuit over the loss of someone's 'dear boy'
The growth of our world leads to the demise of society
Through the lack of vital variety.

Rory Evans (13)
St Birinus' School, Didcot

The Assassin

The bombs screech through the air with devastating hate,
Preparing for the death of hundreds of innocent watchers,
While they acknowledge the upcoming events,
They run to nowhere which is safe,
Only to be consumed by the roaring explosion and heat,
Their deaths were unnecessary, only the man wanted survived,
The corpses scattered over the rubble were consumed by holyness
As the souls departed into the unknown step in life,
To which they killed for a man who survived,
A man whose power is destroyed,
A man who could murder to make a living,
But be safe wherever he walked,
A man whose power could be taken away so easily,
Yet he shall live on with determination.

Joel Elkins (13)
St Birinus' School, Didcot

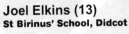

 188

Snowdrops

Snowdrops
Floating, gliding
Dropping, falling
Landing.

The softened land transformed into a cloud.
Children's laughter crystal clear as the ice on the frozen lakes.
The world slows down as pure white, the earth shrouds.
Nature recaptures the earth, the world gently wakes
'Put your wellies on, we're going to the hill,
We'll sledge down the mountainside, we'll do it for the thrill.'
Schools are shut, carols are sung,
Snowmen are made, church bells are rung . . .

    Snowdrops.

James Locke (14)
St Birinus' School, Didcot

My Hill

Lying, waiting, lying, waiting, staring into the eternal beyond
Of the blue grey-sky, symmetrically parallel to the vast carpet
Of patchwork-like fields and meandering streams,
Each reflecting either a magnificent glint of the domineering sun
Or the deep indigo of the coming storm.
I lie viewing this from my fort, my castle, my stronghold of
internal security.
This is my hill, my guardian and my shepherd,
Both with its own supreme power, divine as one,
Allowing me to share its stance on life and infinite youth.
This is my hill, just mine . . .

George Howe (13)
St Birinus' School, Didcot

The Wall

Sitting, staring, bored, blank pages staring me back
Mind empty, extremely numb, forever I sit and wait
Watching my energy move, my thoughts thrown out in a sack
So now this wall cannot be climbed, now this poem meets its safe
Sitting here in the dark, nothing on my mind, a wall in my tracks
Continuous objector to the war in my mind, my thoughts,
no peaceful state
So now I sit here dark and glum, it's only creativity that I lack.

Joe Parker (14)
St Birinus' School, Didcot

The Terrorist Poem

He is a small, stumpy, fat man.
The orphan kid is watching him.
He looks too suspicious!

He goes into the market.
Stands in the middle.
Anger, all over his face.
The orphan follows with pace.

He rips open his jacket and shouts . . .
'Ardejacabar!'
The orphan's eyes full of fear.
The terrorist doesn't even shed a tear.

Boom! Boom! Boom!
The market goes.
Blows away all the hoes.

All for holy reasons.
Sancta simplicitas.

George Watts (13)
St Joseph's College, Ipswich

190

Unlike The People

Wars about religion,
Wars about the land,
Wars about a crusade,
Wars about the sea.

People losing legs,
People losing heads,
People always dying,
Even while they're flying.

Out there in the trenches,
Out there in the sky,
Out there on the sea,
It's suicide going free.

Boats are always sinking,
Great minds always thinking,
It's these men that aren't dying
Unlike all those people out there flying.

Errol Thompson (13)
St Joseph's College, Ipswich

War

The horrible feelings come
Soldier's injury
Screaming around all the place
End of the time
I am fine
All people dead
Makes me cry
Don't want to be lonely
But I am the only.

Jonathan Mo (14)
St Joseph's College, Ipswich

Strawberries And Cream

You and me go together like strawberries and cream.
Love is the feeling in my heart.
I love you more than I love chips,
And I love chips so very much.
I think you and me should go out for tea,
And then maybe end up here.
Then we could laugh and have another beer.
Because you and me go together like strawberries and cream.

Ross Parry (14)
St Joseph's College, Ipswich

Trench Warfare

Bang, bang, bang, bang!
Boom, boom, boom, boom!
That is all you hear in this small and dirty room.

The guns are firing and the birds are dying.
From every bullet fired, a soldier's death is inevitable.

Here they climb over the trench and enter the wretched hell zone.
The drums of war thunder, once again!

Sam Jenner (13)
St Joseph's College, Ipswich

All I Ask

As her head lies in my arms,
Her bright blue eyes alight.

She smiles a smile and laughs a laugh,
Her dark brown curls a shine.

The peach-soft skin all soft and smooth,
Her plump, soft hands so small.

All I ask is just one last thing,
Make this last until morn.

Emily Brighty (13)
Scaltback Middle School, Newmarket

192

The Lady Of Shalott

Gazing down from her tower, pretty as a new sprung flower,
Stood a woman seeking power.
Stayed there every single hour,
        Fair maiden of Camelot.
There she looked at the mirror, reflecting the sky even clearer.
There she sees the knight come nearer,
        The Lady of Shalott.

In her room there she stay, with a curse night and day.
On her bed there she lay, in her tower there she say,
    'I'm trapped in towered Camelot.'
There she feels cast off, alone, in a prison on her own.
In the room made of stone,
        The Lady of Shalott.

Sir Lancelot heard her voice calling, even when it wasn't morning,
She caught a glimpse when day was dawning,
The curse was on without a warning,
        There she screamed at Camelot.
There she ran from her room,
To escape the curse of doom.
From her life of long gloom,
        The Lady of Shalott.

To follow the knight, her true love,
From her tower up above.
There she sees a white dove,
Which represents the heart of love.
        Flying down to Camelot.
There she tripped and hit the ground,
Darkness growing all around,
She lays with hope for a sound.
        Trapped is The Lady of Shalott.

Emily Allen (11)
Scaltback Middle School, Newmarket

Funny School Poem

Drama is fun
Like a beat of a drum.
History's boring
I can't stop yawning.
Science is experimental
And I find my teacher very helpful.
Music is loud,
You can hear it in the clouds.
I love information technology,
But I'd rather learn biology.
Geography is confusing
I don't find it amusing.
Religious education
Is worthwhile
And full of information.
DT is not that great
But I do get to sit with my mates.
PE is fun,
Especially when I run.
English is great,
So don't be late.
French is a bit hazy,
But my mum said it's because I'm lazy.
Maths is alright
If you can add and you're bright.
Art is creative,
Especially when I'm painting.
You may not like school,
But you'll grow up and be cool!

Zoe Jaggard (11)
Scaltback Middle School, Newmarket

The Captain

The captain stood on the ship
By stillness it was consumed
When a breeze picked up and the boat was struck
In Africa they were marooned.

A whale appeared right near the boat
A man shot out of its spout
With a moan and a groan he got back up
He was blind with no eyes to see out.

The men said, 'Go west my friends,'
The crew was shocked, but didn't disobey
It had been five days but now they could see land
All the crews' fears did allay.

They would reach land by morning
The captain went and rested
He had a dream the man would kill him,
He entered the room where the man had nested.

He plunged the dagger through his chest
With a gurgle he took his last breath
The captain looked back to see his grim deed
Choking in pain the man met his death.

The captain was relieved after his deed
But there broke a vicious storm,
When the curse was revealed
His men were all gone.

Ben Manchett (12)
Scaltback Middle School, Newmarket

Trust

Trust is like a mountain -
It is a long way to the top
But it's worth the uphill climb.

Rhiannon McBean (12)
Scaltback Middle School, Newmarket

195

Fields Of Flame

That November day that needs no name
Represented by the fields of flame.
It makes me think of years before,
Of men that lost their lives to war.

The young, the old and the barely new,
Doing what they're told to do.
Nine foot down and all alone,
Within the trench they now call home.

As bullets flew through the air,
They advanced without a care.
A hail of bullets, the sound of a bomb,
Their shattered bodies upon the Somme.

A second war upon us came,
The same enemy with a different name.
The children cried at their mother's knees,
While their fathers fought for liberty.

Challenged again to fight the duel,
Of living under Nazi rule.
Korean, Falklands and now as before,
Young men still being called to war.

We wear a poppy to show our pride.
To honour the men that have given their lives.
We may not know them all by name,
But we all wear a flower from the fields of fame.

Ashleigh Gates (12)
Scaltback Middle School, Newmarket

Forgiveness Or Retribution

If you seek retribution
In an act of blinding anger,
Step out of the picture - just to look,
Because revenge you may seek no longer

Once you seek too far in revenge,
It is hard to escape
The torture and the panic
That it has left in its wake.

By carrying on this pretence
You get hurt inside.
Mentally - not physically, and by yourself, no other,
By the past and what is left behind.

No one can change events,
Just like a withering flower
Once it has gone, it can't come back,
But you can learn from its influencing power.

It's then when you wish you hadn't done it
When you can turn around and walk away
It's now that you have learnt to forgive
And that you can walk up the stairway.

Jessica Walton (12)
Scaltback Middle School, Newmarket

Passing Moment

I'm lying in a field dreaming up into Heaven,
Wishing that you were lying here with me,
Just one more minute to hear your voice again
But now you're resting and not in pain.
Why did you have to go so soon? I'm asking
Goodbye my butterfly, I'll see you one day . . .

Abbie Jenkins (12)
Scaltback Middle School, Newmarket

197

Forgiveness

Forgiveness is like a road.
You take the wrong turn and you come to a dead end.
Sometimes it can be hard to turn around,
Go back and start all over again.
All you want to do is stay where you are and stay there forever.
Forever getting older.
Forever trapped.
Trapped in your thoughts haunting your own world.

But if you keep going straight
You will find happiness some day.
If you learn to forgive and forget
You will find God was always on your side.

However if you seek revenge you will end up being just like them.
Trapped
Trapped with a forever heavy burden.
Never giving you a break.
Never . . .
Ever . . .

Alice Goodridge (13)
Scaltback Middle School, Newmarket

Forgiveness Poem

Forgiveness is like the ocean, rough at the beginning
But can become calm.
Forgiveness can be hard but it is rewarding.
Forgiveness is like a team sport, hard to co-operate
But when you do it, it can work in your favour
If you forgive others then they will forgive you.

Josh Marks (12)
Scaltback Middle School, Newmarket

The Many Forms Of Love

Love is like a snowflake.
Delicate, light, precious.
But it may not last forever
It will melt, disappear and then it shall be gone.

Love is like a fire.
It will start with a few minute sparks,
But will ascend into a healthy flame.
Although you may think the roaring fire is strong,
It can be extinguished.

That is the beauty,
The intelligence of love.
It sneaks into your life and you are overjoyed.
Then it is crushed, torn, stabbed and it just fades away
Into the pallid moonlight of the still night,
Where nothing stirs, nothing quakes
And love is gone.

Charlotte Grass (12)
Scaltback Middle School, Newmarket

The Bashing Bank Robbery

With guns held high, they kicked open the bank's door.
They stole from the rich, they stole from the poor.
Grabbing their black hand guns, they quickly aimed.
With chattering teeth
Lurking beneath
The cold and dusty stairs
Poor ladies screamed and cried,
Children shouted, 'It's not fair,' and they wiped their mum's tears dry.
With guns held high the police ran in,
Ready to get 'em in the bin.
The robbers tiptoed out
And without a doubt
The robbers won't be about.

Shannon Day (11)
Scaltback Middle School, Newmarket

The Man From Bangkok

A one-legged man from Bangkok
Had a very smelly sock
He smelt it one day
And fainted away
And hit his head on a rock.

He woke up in a hospital bed
With a manky bandage on his head
He picked up some toast
And then saw is ghost
On that cold toasted bread.

It was time for him to go home
But his house was in a dome.
So then he went in
And saw in his bin
His cat eating his shaving foam.

Josh Conlon (11)
Scaltback Middle School, Newmarket

Three Words

How can I forgive when I'm feeling like this?
Wrapped up in hate, enclosed in this cycle
Round and round, never ending,
Help! I need someone to pull me out.
My mind is focussed on punishing the perpetrator.
I can't walk in that room and say it,
I push out, breathe in
I won't look back, won't give in.
The door's open, I confidently stride in,
'I forgive you.'
Those three words are said too often but not enough,
He listened and nodded,
'I'm sorry.'

Kate McGrath (13)
Scaltback Middle School, Newmarket

2oo

Love And Hatred

Love is like an ocean.
It's soft but yet still very cold.
Love is like an ocean because it never ends.

Hatred is like a fire - hot but still very hurtful.
Fire is hurtful like you can hurt yourself.

Bethany Mary Ann Bell (12)
Scaltback Middle School, Newmarket

Reflections

I look in the mirror
And all I see
Is a girl I don't know
Staring back at me.

Who am I?
What am I?
I'm not sure
I've never seen myself before.

I'm just a girl
With a big fake smile,
I haven't looked inside,
Not for a while.

I want to know,
I want to see,
I want to be confident -
Confident in me.

But I do know this: I can be
Anything or anyone I want to be.
I want to be myself,
I want to be free,
I want to look inside,
I want to know me.

Jodie Brown (14)
Stalham High School, Stalham

201

From Future To Myth

We have all seen future become past;
Things come and things go.
Sometimes they go just too fast,
Yet sometimes just too slow.

We have all seen past become history,
The bow and arrow came and went;
Now it's part of a children's story,
But still off to war our boys are sent

We have all seen history become legend.
The ancients gave a mysterious warning;
We all fear Armageddon, the world's end.
In distant cities bombs fall, night and morning.

We have all seen legend become myth,
Tales of gods no longer exists,
They died out while people still live
And biased leadership we still resist.

Calvin Waters (13)
Stalham High School, Stalham

Nintendo DS

Great
For when
It's boring
Play anywhere
If I should lose it
I'd be really upset
But then I'd steal my brother's
And play racing games once again.

Sam Hampshire (14)
Stalham High School, Stalham

I See You

I see you. Crossing the high street
A nervous giggle, just for me.
You've brought your friends for company, protection
To hide from my affection
But I don't want them,
It's only you and my infatuation
My eternal adoration
Pining for a long-lasting, lip-locking romance
That will never die
Or fade away or just pass by.

I see you. Living that mundane life, only I can brighten
No need to be frightened
You took a restraining order
Just more of a challenge
A chance for my talents,
A chance to shine.

I see you. Some will say it's tragic
I take the knife, my form of magic
Always one for dramatics
They call me a fanatic
But my fierce love will last forever,
So take my hand baby, and we'll leave this world together.

Daniel Griffiths (15)
The Forest School, Horsham

The Wind Blows And Blows And Blows

The wind blows and blows and blows.
The trees bend, the chairs fly,
One lone boy starts to cry.

Houses fall, people run,
One single man, one single gun.

His wife is dead, all hope lost,
Two shots. Another life gone.
A single man no more.

People jump, people dodge
Shrapnel falls like rain
Over the hills, under the cloud barrier,
Dust and smoke fill their lungs.

The wind has died, the rubble stayed.
We clean up bodies frayed,
Until hope comes, people fear,
The wind that blows and blows . . .

Owen Hayles (13)
The Forest School, Horsham

Ice Mountain

The snowflakes furiously swarm in their billions.
The harsh wind slaps your raw cheek.
It is graceful yet brutal,
Majestic, yet deadly,
So strong, it could never be weak.

The glaciers are slowly slipping;
The mountains enjoying their sleep.
The caves in the ice
Are hiding away
From the beauty of the
Mountain peak.

Tanya Lang (13)
The Leys School, Cambridge

204

Failure

You're a very intelligent woman, they say,
We think you could go to Oxbridge,
If you work and study hard every day.
So I work, and I work, and I work, and I work.
For I must keep on achieving,
Because I know how disappointment hurts.

I work all through every day and night,
I must keep working and working
To keep success within my sights.
I have no time for life; I have no time to live,
But living doesn't matter to me,
Because success is all there is.

And God! Oh God, how failure scares me,
It shows me disappointed faces,
And all the things that I might not be.
Nobody else understands why I'm scared;
It doesn't seem to bother them
That the possibility is always there.

So I set myself standards impossibly high,
And I know I never can reach them.
Yet still, I try and I try and I try and I try,
The fear of failure urges me on,
And the desire for success engulfs me,
Until all other feeling is gone.

It leaves me alone, but they tell me not to care.
You don't need love to be successful,
Because it doesn't get you anywhere.
Friendships will fade and may leave you in tears
But success has greater worth,
As it will last a thousand years.

And I've been working for so very long
That I've never really known love;
So I'll never know if they're wrong.

Florence Hyde (15)
The Leys School, Cambridge

205

My Ballad

Florence and the Machine,
Quite a strange name,
In the past few years
She has made her claims to fame.

Her alternative genre
And her wild red hair,
Whenever she walks by,
You see people stare.

She's good at singing,
Don't you think?
It shows in her songs,
That she'll never sink.

Florence and the Machine
Quite a strange name,
Some may not think her good,
But I like her all the same.

Her debut album,
Lungs it was called
I have to say, it left the critics
Rather appalled.

A rising star she was that day,
When she burst out of her shell,
So many people bought that album,
(And listened to it as well)

She's made many songs,
All for work and money,
With her invisible machine,
The outlook's always sunny.

Her strange voice it has to be said,
Echoes through the room,
Even though it's quite dark outside,
It still uplifts the gloom.

I enjoy her music,
It makes me smile,
Listening to it,
Is really worthwhile.

Florence and the Machine,
Quite a strange name,
I like her a lot,
Because her hair is like a flame.

Edward Penty (11)
The Leys School, Cambridge

His Majesty, Deluded

Cut me; scar me. My skin is soft.
Strike me; bruise me. My flesh is ripe.
Rip me; slash me open. I bleed.
Beat me; break me; choke me. Strip me
Of all honour, virtue, hope and love;
But you will never kill me.
Your hate cannot destroy me;
Your weapons cannot make me die.

What is death to me? I am the fire
And the fire burns within me. I am
The monarch of the ancient stars,
The uncrowned king of dust and gold.
My lustre will not fade with time;
I shall not kneel to death, nor die.

Alexander John Mitchell Greaves (17)
The Leys School, Cambridge

The Furniture Dance

Said the lamp to the mirror, 'My dearest sweet, can I take you to the dance?'
She looked at him with her sparkling eyes and said, 'There's not a chance! I'm to go with a real gentleman, the fairest in the land!'
'And who may that be?' the lamp enquired.
'Oh the darling music stand.'
'It's true he may be great and fair and an honour to walk by his side, but surely he cannot make you feel as warm or bright inside?'
But the mirror was stubborn - 'The music stand has won the whole of my heart, and neither you nor the brightest of lamps could tear us two apart.'

On the night of the dance how the lamp did weep and his bulb dulled right down,
for he knew no fairer girl was seen in the whole of that little town.
But suddenly his bulb shone again in the brightest tone,
for a beautiful curtain came wandering by, so sad and so alone.
'My dear,' he cried, 'have you no one to dance with at the ball?'
'I was to go with the shelf,' she said, 'but he's too attached to the wall!'
The lamp shone bright, 'Well come with me for I have no one at all, and we shall show the shelf who he should have gone with to the ball.'

Together they danced to the music of Handel, the greatest of all doorknobs,
and soon they pranced out into the open, away from the noisy mops.
A breeze came by and curtain swayed, so soft in Lamps embrace,
and Curtain twirled around and round with such a beautiful grace.
They danced and danced and Curtain smiled and Lamp shone like a torch.
And under the stars and the shining moon they kissed upon the porch.

Hannah Bowen (14)
The Leys School, Cambridge

 **2o8**

Untitled

Here where John Betjeman lies
In the churchyard of St Enodoc
Far from the city, far from the town, a country mouse am I
No noise, no hustle and bustle like the town
The vicar weekly pops around to check that all is sound
Around the pews and altar where I live
The cleaners come dusting and polishing
With polish that tastes like jam!
They bring with them biscuits to snack on with tea
A quick dash while their backs are turned to share in their
tasty delights.
The summer is best when the tourists come to view
The poet laureate, John Betjeman's stone
He wrote poems about all things in life
'Diary of a Church Mouse', that's about my father
Life in town was too much to bear
So he jumped into the back of John Betjeman's car
Down to his house beside the sea
To Trebetherick he came
He lived under the warm floorboards
Collecting all sorts for his lovely new house.
He met his new neighbour
And married her quick!
When Harvest time came, the patter of feet
Brothers, sisters and I
Lovely seasons we had, lots of fun was shared
But then a terrible thing happened . . .
John Betjeman died . . .
New owners moved in
And bought a cat, which caught old dad . . .
We moved out quick to St Enodoc Church and next to JB he lies,
In a plot in the churchyard.

Jemima Acock (12)
Uplands Community College, Wadhurst

The Beast

The click, the flash,
The quicker you go,
The quicker you get away,
From the beast that waits.

Run through the forest,
Into the mist,
Far away,
And leave it behind.

Reaching the moment you get lost,
To the time you make up your mind,
And away into the darkness,
To find the truth lies ahead.

Suddenly the noise grows,
The tension starts to build,
And you find out,
That it's just there.

Run or stay, stay or run,
You must decide,
Stay or run, run or stay,
You think what to do now.

The light appears in front,
You charge straight at it,
The thoughts evaporate,
Into the misty forest.

Running, running,
Away, away
Your imagination brings you home,
Open the door and there it is, the beast.

Jessie Rosenberg (12)
Uplands Community College, Wadhurst

210

The Football Game

Today is the day of the big match
My time to shine
I stand on the fresh green grass
I wait nervously for the whistle
I wait for a minute
The ref blows
The game is underway
After five minutes the game gets going
A long ball to the left mid, the ball is mine
I run for a bit
I am around one person, and another
Then in my way is a six-foot-tall giant
He stands like a rock
He is hairy
Smelly
And very big
I look around left then right
Then the winger runs next to me
A quick one two, I'm away
One on one with keeper, I can't miss
I take a breath and run
I shoot, *bang,*
Goal!
I'm in the team.

Thomas Buckingham (11)
Uplands Community College, Wadhurst

Snow

The white blankets cover the empty fields,
A fresh fall adds to the crusty top,
The slate roofs become completely white,
Soon it will be gone,
While it falls, no one stirs.

Fred Newson (12)
Uplands Community College, Wadhurst

The Mind Of A Madman

All the demons and paranoia,
Forgotten names and dates.
Movie titles and holidays,
And trains arriving late.
Timetables for nothing,
And hopes crouched in the dark.
The nightmares and the tears,
Circling like sharks.
The love of a mother,
The laugh of a friend.
All of those meetings,
You have to attend.
Screams from the darkness,
And cries in the night.
The fear of growing old,
And losing your sight.
Faintly shining moonlight,
And clouds rolling in.
The mind of a madman,
Troubled by his sin.

Alex Rostron (12)
Uplands Community College, Wadhurst

The Cheetah

Sleek, shiny
Covered with spots
Hidden by the dappled light
Comes the cheetah.

Creeping through the bushes
He stops and listens
Crouched coiled to spring . . .

A scream shatters the moonlight
The cheetah has struck
Again.

Georgie Hart (11)
Uplands Community College, Wadhurst

212

If I Were . . .

If I were a dog,
I would dig a hole ten feet deep.
If I were a cloud,
I would make it sleet.
If I were a celebrity,
I would shoo everyone away.
If I were a referee,
I would make it fair play.
But . . .
If I were the Queen,
I would stop the war.
If I were rich,
I would pay the poor.
If I were Mother Nature,
I would stop bad crops.
If I were important,
I would make everyone tops!

If I were God,
I would . . .

Charlotte Turner (11)
Uplands Community College, Wadhurst

Butterfly!

Butterfly, butterfly,
Flying in the deep blue sky,
Dancing in the wind.
Your elegant wings flapping,
The patterns shining.
The brown upon your wings,
The blue upon the plants,
You combine the colours to make one.
Standing out upon all,
You're the only one,
Butterfly, butterfly.

Jasmin Claassens-Dussek (11)
Uplands Community College, Wadhurst

213

Year Sevens!

When the sixth formers are standing tall,
The little Year 7s are staying small,
And when it comes to the football,
The Year 7s have no chance at all.

It's very hard to believe,
What Year 7s manage to achieve.
I know this might make you grieve
But cute Year 7s do deceive.

When they enter into lessons,
They come out with some frightening confessions!
The girls talk so much about fashion,
You would think it was their only passion!

You may think those Year 7s are very mad,
And it may make you very sad,
But really you should be so glad,
Because they aren't all that bad!

Sophie Macleod (12)
Uplands Community College, Wadhurst

Cat's Affection

C ats are fast and curious
A gile as they walk
T hey are independent and comforting
S ly as they pounce on the unknown piece of thread.

A s you stare at their glistening eyes
F or you wish they could speak
F orever springing onto your lap
E very time they flop to the floor
C ompanions for life
T hey are there when you're happy or sad
I n your heart that's where they will be
O n the kitchen table or on your favourite chair
N ever will they leave you.

Emma Williams (12)
Uplands Community College, Wadhurst

When I Was Younger

When I was five
I loved to live.
I always was a pain
My mother said to me one day, 'We're going on a plane.'

I wondered what the plane was like
I wondered whether I could take my bike.
I couldn't sleep at all that night
Wondering whether the plane had lights.

We got in my auntie's car
I hurt myself on her towbar
My brother he was flicking me
My mother said, 'Let her be.'

The plane as busy as could be
My father got scared of losing me
I ate a sweet
Because I wanted to eat.

Annabel Stevenson (11)
Uplands Community College, Wadhurst

Falling Star

I look up at the night sky, ever so dark,
Gazing at the bright stars as they shine,
But one quick flash and it's all gone,
A falling star is all I see.

I can't take my eyes off this wonderful sight,
Oh, what a view, I'm not going to move,
I've never seen anything like it before,
But oh, I wish I had.

I close my eyes and make a wish,
What shall I wish for? Let me think,
Just one more minute it will be alright.

Too late, my falling star is gone.

Gabbie Marsh (11)
Uplands Community College, Wadhurst

215

New

I walk into my new classroom,
Eyes staring at me like there is something wrong,
All I want to do is make friends,
But everyone I speak to laughs at me,
Maybe I just don't fit in here.

I walk into my new classroom,
My teacher gets my name wrong,
I sit in the wrong seat,
I bump into the head cheerleader,
What else can go wrong?

I walk into my new classroom,
Girls in their cliques talking about me,
Boys looking me up and down,
I'm just new,
They were new once,
What have I done wrong?

Brontë King (12)
Uplands Community College, Wadhurst

Life

Friendship is for memorable moments,
For the party worth living,
For the hours of laughter,
For the generous giving,

Love is for soul,
For life,
And for songs,
Love is for falling,
Forgiving the wrong.

Life is for love,
For plenty of friendship,
For giving your all,
And lasting forever.

Hannah Wedge (13)
Uplands Community College, Wadhurst

To Live

Glancing at the drops of rain,
Falling from the sky,
Sitting at my window pane,
All I want to do is cry,
That groping feeling in my mind
Settled in my head,
So many empty thoughts, my mind has gone blind,
Lost all of his words right now, can't remember what he said,
That recurring thought flowing through my mind,
Of the day I'll always dread,
That sudden feeling in my heart.
Struck me like a bullet,
All I can remember is his cold and frail face,
All I can remember is the breath of a dying man,
And all I can remember is the longing in his eyes,
His life was meant to live.

Rosa Jackson (13)
Uplands Community College, Wadhurst

The Hunter

Twinkling in the sky were golden stars
And in the distance, you could hear the murmur of cars.
Like guards stood the pines, sturdy and tall.
Through the emerald leaves came a pigeon's call.

A sleek cat crept through the trees
His midnight-black coat ruffled in the breeze.
Under his chin lay a patch of snow-white fur
And out of his dagger-sharp teeth came an almost silent purr.
His glowing green eyes were wide and bright
As he stalked his prey throughout the night.

Through the shadows he weaved and danced
Along the hillside he advanced.
And with one quick movement, a swipe of his claws
The dance was over with the snap of his jaws.

Frankie Jolliffe (11)
Uplands Community College, Wadhurst

217

Storm

The wind blows through the trees,
The rain splats on the leaves,
The clouds sigh,
In the grey sky,
As I watch them crying over me.

I walk up to the sea front,
The sea is harsh and cold,
The pebbles clank,
As my foot sank,
Water is surrounding me.

People run for cover,
As the rain hits down harder,
But I roam free,
Completely carefree,
In the storm of never-ending water.

Morgan Wagg (12)
Uplands Community College, Wadhurst

Perfect

So many brilliant ideas,
But when you see them on paper you realise how ridiculous they are
You try a different one,
'But how do I start this?'
Childhood?
Your first holiday? How about your friends?
Friends, yes, that could work
Put it to paper . . . oh, same problem, it sounds so dull.
But then you get a flash of inspiration.
A bright idea,
'That's what I'll do.'
From then on it comes out like you're talking to your best friend
Flows so effortlessly
Like the language you've spoken all your life.
This poem is *perfect*.

Beth Lanham (11)
Uplands Community College, Wadhurst

218

Gramps

Gramps was a funny old fella,
He had a dog he loved called Bella,
A true Chelsea man,
I think he's their number one fan.

He also plays football in the garden with me,
But quickly got tired and wanted his tea,
A hanky in his pocket, Polos too,
Just to share with me and a special few.

An Easter egg hunt was our yearly treat,
But forgot where he hid them it was a hard task to meet.

We went down the coast to get an ice cream
'99 flake please' we all used to scream.

I'll miss you Gramps, and love you forever,
But don't forget to say hi to Bella.

Sam Newton (13)
Uplands Community College, Wadhurst

Mum Is Having A Baby!

Mum is having a baby,
I'm scared,
I'm worried,
I don't know what to do,
And I'm lying in bed thinking . . .
What's the matter with me?
I mean, I'm . . .
Funny,
Smart,
Caring,
Charming,
And most of all,
I never moan about eating,
Soggy spinach,
If you read this Mum, spinach is *yuck!*

Ben Sayer (11)
Uplands Community College, Wadhurst

219

Global Warming

Hot, hot, how hot can I go,
Hot, it's humid and sticky, we need to go.
Do you know why? It's us you see,
It's going to get hotter and hotter if this carries on,
So make it stop or everyone will suffer,
Doves and dogs and reptiles too!
Will you let them suffer from our problems?
Think about who will die, not only us but the animals too.
They welcomed us on Earth, so we should respect them as we
respect ourselves.
Don't let this happen it is a beautiful planet,
We still have time to make a difference,
For you and you and them.

Ben Farebrother (11)
Uplands Community College, Wadhurst

Giraffe

With its head in the sky,
Watching the world flutter on by.
You just stand waiting . . . waiting
Then suddenly you look at me

With your light brown eyes,
The same as twenty spies,
Watching me carefully . . . softly
And as I advance, you come closer

Just like a champion poser,
I feel I need to bend my neck
Because, giraffe
You are my best friend.

Emily Clary (11)
Uplands Community College, Wadhurst

220

Time

Speeding up when I'm in a hurry
Late for something
All I do is constantly worry
Got to be sharp and right on time
The clock is ticking
I'm wasting every minute of this precious time.

Waiting patiently as the day goes on
Slowing down
What else could go wrong?
I want to go home
Go home and be gone
Why is this time taking so long?

Amber Twiner (11)
Uplands Community College, Wadhurst

Piano

I walk to the stage.
I stare at the empty auditorium.
No sound.
No movement.
Just nothing.
I take my seat on the cold leather stool.
My hand touches the smooth ivory keys.
My feet rest on the shiny bronze pedals.
I press one key and the high-pitched note echoes
Around the arena.
Silence.
And I begin.

Callum Helliwell (13)
Uplands Community College, Wadhurst

Snow

Snow is so white,
Snow is so deep.
It is so bright,
I need to sleep.

It glistens in the sun,
Melting very slowly.
I am having fun,
But I am very lonely.

I am making a snowman,
To help me on my way
My best wish is to make it snow every day.

Emily Colley (12)
Uplands Community College, Wadhurst

The Race Of The Wii

I raced to the Wii and turned it on,
Got a snack, a large scone,
The screen was loading,
Loading, still loading,
Come on!
I urged it to start,
Finally it was there,
My favourite game,
Here again,
Every day,
I'm never ever going away.

Jonathan Seakins (11)
Uplands Community College, Wadhurst

222

The Mountain Of The World Spirit
(Based on the book 'Wolf Brother')

It was menacing.
The mountain.
It rose higher than the
Highest cloud.
And even then, it climbed.

He had travelled all this way
For the impossible climb.
He was afraid to fail
His dad and himself.

Elliot Hayward (12)
Uplands Community College, Wadhurst

Snowy Days

Snowy days are just the best
They get me into my thermal vest
I gaze out the window and can't believe what I see
I see the white stuff and I'm filled with glee.
My mum tells me there is no school
And I think that is just so cool.
I grab my sledge and off I go
Running and sliding in the snow!
Fighting in it is brilliant fun
But now sadly, here comes the sun!

Billy Farris (11)
Uplands Community College, Wadhurst

Time

Time is like a good dream, you never want it to end
Time is like a fortress, it cannot be penetrated
Time is alive, it can be good or bad, pleasant or wicked
Time is a blazing fire, it can change in an instant

Dan Money (12)
Uplands Community College, Wadhurst

223

Twilight

One stormy, gloomy night one wolf came out to fight,
One wolf here, one wolf there, you're never going to stop them
So you may as well give up.
A vampire comes and the werewolf goes
That's how you get rid of one of those!

If you ever see one don't be afraid
Just think of this rhyme and you will see the best will happen
To these who wait.

Teagan Lilly-Moore (11)
Uplands Community College, Wadhurst

The Moon

I am round yet large
I reflect the light
Many people have visited me
Yet many dream of doing so
To eat the cheese that I am made
Visitors have a great story to tell
When they have walked on my crust
What a tale to tell.

Reece Lyons (13)
Uplands Community College, Wadhurst

Cheese

Cheesy puffs are the best,
I just don't like all the rest,
Cheddar, brie and Swiss,
Eating them is just bliss,
Crackers with a slice of cheese,
Oh yes they really do appease,
Cheddar, brie and Swiss,
Eating them is just bliss.

Carl Gamage (11)
Uplands Community College, Wadhurst

Grandpa

Grandpa is a friend
A shoulder to cry on
A soulmate for life
A hug when you need it most
He makes me smile when I feel down
A forever child
Telling stories and memorable ones too
And a best friend for life.

Sophie Tate (11)
Uplands Community College, Wadhurst

The Loss

Her misted lonely eyes,
Stare longingly into mine.
The tears that trickle down,
It's a cycle that goes round and round.
Her withered, frail hands,
Caress my flooded cheeks.
Yet soon she will land,
It's Heaven's door she'll meet.

Natalie Barden (13)
Uplands Community College, Wadhurst

Life

Life is a dream of which we all want to obtain
Life is a burden separating us, making us different
Life is worth living but not at the peril of another
Life can be lost at the hands of fate
Life is lost and no hope lies ahead
Only darkness and grief remain
Life is a dream in which we all lose
So let's leave that way because we can't choose.

Adam Packham (13)
Uplands Community College, Wadhurst

225

Lonely In The Dark

Lonely in the dark,
Lonely in the midnight sky
Lonely as you watch the foil
Lie stars, lonely as you
Listen to babblin' brooks, lonely
Sitting peaceful in the heart of
The darkness, lonely in the dark.

Olivia Charles (12)
Uplands Community College, Wadhurst

A Part Of Life

School time is upon us,
It is a time to meet people, friends, followers.
It's days upon days of learning,
Memories are created
Days can be full of ups and down.
But in the end . . .
You'll never forget it's a part of life.

Maisie Thomas (13)
Uplands Community College, Wadhurst

New Coat Of Paint

Making a promise is like throwing a handful of sand up in the air.
You can't expect to catch it all.
Life is like dropping a feather to the ground,
Just as it's about to touch the floor you can't help but pick it up again.

And love is like painting a rusty gate,
It looks fine for a few years, but before you know it,
You'll end up right where you started,
Except this time, it'll be worse than before.
But it can always be painted over again.

Lydia Granger (11)
Wood Green School, Witney

The Age Of Foes

Daylight burns, but I recall
When candlelight flickered on Winnie's fur.
Days may fly on silver wings,
But I can still remember
Swaying in the oak to save it from the axe.
Weeks gallop by on four hard hooves,
But I remember Nid the Clown
Flying kites on Elvin Mound.

That was before the age of foes,
The age of cars, the age of woes.
That was before the age of wars,
The age of guns, the age of swords.
This age when time regrets our love.

Months float by like clouds above,
But I still hear the songs we sang,
The jokes we told, the tales we shared.
Years glide fast on witches' brooms
But I recall our hide-and-seek, our friendly talk.
And as the whole world blindly falls,
I remember those who cared.

That was before the DVDs.
Computer games and MP3s.
The age of violence, gloom and strife.
That was before the mobile phones,
TVs and computer zones,
The age of time, the thief of life.

Evie Telford-Moore (14)
Wood Green School, Witney

Frozen Actress

I've seen pain in your eyes
And I don't care
This is nothing but fake despair
You lure them in
And tear them apart
Just to gain an unfrozen heart
You shed a tear
To make a scene
An unannounced drama queen
You plant a smile on an unlucky guy
And leave his heart in the shape to die
What is it like to be an empty vase?
Where no one can see through
Look in your heart
And what do you see?
A life of pain and misery.

Andrew Jones (14)
Wood Green School, Witney

Tears Of Love

Raindrops are tears of love.
Love that has been killed and lost,
Love that many have been waiting for,
Love that is still crying,
And most of all still killing;
No wonder why there's so much.

Zoe Fabian (12)
Wood Green School, Witney

228

Young Writers Information

We hope you have enjoyed reading this book - and that you will continue to enjoy it in the coming years.

If you like reading and writing poetry drop us a line, or give us a call, and we'll send you a free information pack.

Alternatively if you would like to order further copies of this book or any of our other titles, then please give us a call or log onto our website at www.youngwriters.co.uk.

Young Writers Information
Remus House
Coltsfoot Drive
Peterborough
PE2 9JX
(01733) 890066